EMPOWERING YOUR HIGHLY SENSITIVE CHILD

A Comprehensive Parent's Guide

by

Millie Thornfield

Cover Design by Angela Alayo
Illustrations by Kanwal Ilyas

First Edition: October 2024

Contents

Chapter 1

INTRODUCTION

"Highly Sensitive Children are the quiet revolutionaries of our time, whose depth of feeling and keen perception hold the key to unlocking a more compassionate and understanding world." - Brene Brown

Have you ever noticed your kid acting a little differently? Maybe you can't quite put your finger on it, but you see them react more intensely to the subtle changes in their environment than others of their age. Your little one is quite bright, intuitive, and in many ways ahead of what you would expect for their age. Yet they struggle with simple routine tasks or can sometimes become upset at the drop of a dime. If this sounds familiar, you might be raising a highly sensitive child.

We all know that parenting is a journey filled with joy, challenges, and countless moments of growth. Yet, for those of us raising Highly Sensitive Children (HSC), this journey can often feel like stepping into uncharted territory especially when we know nothing about how to raise a highly sensitive kid. This path is loaded with uncertainties and unique struggles. If you are holding this book in your hands, chances are you have felt the weight of these challenges firsthand. You may have experienced the ache of seeing your child misunderstood or stigmatized by society and you yearn for a world that appreciates their unique qualities rather than labeling them as different or strange. Maybe you've wrestled with the desire to nurture a well-adjusted, happy, and confident child, despite the hurdles posed by their sensitivity. Or you have found yourself at a loss, overwhelmed by the intensity of your child's emotions and reactions.

If that's the case, then this guidebook comes as a perfect read for you. In these pages, you will find solace, understanding, and practical guidance designed specifically for parents like you, who are raising Highly Sensitive Children. This book is not just another parenting manual; rather, it is a roadmap created with empathy and expertise that will empower you to steer through the unique terrain of parenting a Highly Sensitive Child.

For many years, as a Family and Parenting Counselor and multi-specialism therapist, I have come across parents worrying about their child's sensitivity and intense emotional reactions. However, with the right guidance and effective strategies, I have seen them overcoming their worries and helping their sensitive kids regulate their emotions and channel their energies in the right direction. After witnessing the initial difficulties and struggles that most parents of Highly Sensitive Children (HSC) face due to a lack of basic awareness, I am here to walk alongside you and provide a comprehensive guide with every little detail there is to know about raising a Highly Sensitive Child, how their minds work and the best approaches to raising them into confident adults.

Throughout these chapters, you will discover helpful strategies that will allow you to acknowledge and cherish your child's sensitivity as a gift rather than a burden. You will learn how to cultivate an environment where your child feels seen, understood, and greatly valued for who they are. From understanding the intricacies of the emotional world of your child to advocating for their needs in various settings, this book is a comprehensive toolkit to support you every step of the way.

First, we will begin by developing a deeper understanding of what it means to be a highly sensitive child. The more you know your child's psychology the easier it gets to comfort them and teach them how to handle their sensitivity. Once you discover the traits of highly sensitive kids, we will delve into the world of emotions to explore the power of emotional intelligence (EQ). When kids develop a high EQ at an early age, they become adept at dealing with their emotions and reactions to different stimuli. In this book, you will discover effective strategies and activities to guide your Highly Sensitive Child along the path of emotional regulation.

But that's not all. There is so much more that will enable you to nurture your child with consistent support and understanding. From ways to protect you and your child from emotional drain to using holistic wellness, diet, good quality sleep, building their confidence and resilience, and other valuable techniques. This guide offers valuable insights that will significantly transform the lives of your young one and your entire family.

While employing all this knowledge, just remember to be patient with them and be kind to yourself as well. Your strength, calm, and composure help them pick up the same demeanor, so take good care of your mental, physical, and emotional well-being throughout this journey to bring the best version of yourself to the table.

BONUS GIFT
Companion Workbook & Journal

As a thank you for purchasing this book, I have a Companion Workbook & Journal as a Bonus Gift, to support the exercises and strategies in the book for you and your Highly Sensitive Child.

Because the book covers a fairly wide age range, you can choose whether to print the whole Workbook or leave out the pages that are not currently age-appropriate for your child.

The first section is for you, as parents going through this journey with your child. It will help you focus your thoughts on the issues discussed in the book.

The little ones can get involved in some fun activities and stay engaged. I recommend printing additional copies of some of the pertinent illustration pages, sticking these on stiff card, and cutting the shapes out. I would also recommend you stick small Velcro dots to the underside of them so they can be used and reused as often as desired.

For an older Highly Sensitive Child, there are exercises and journaling pages with prompts to help them focus their thoughts and provide them with talking points for you both.

To claim your Gift, please scan this QR code:

Chapter 2

UNDERSTANDING YOUR HIGHLY SENSITIVE CHILD

"Highly sensitive children are the future's peacemakers. They feel deeply, and their compassion will change the world." — Elaine N. Aron

Every time I meet parents raising a Highly Sensitive Child, I congratulate them for bringing such a compassionate being into this world. HSCs are indeed different from most kids of their age and that's what makes them highly unique and valuable. When raised with a balance of love, care, and emotional intelligence, these kids grow up to be highly confident, composed, and successful adults. Since their minds work differently, you need a little help to understand them better and employ parenting techniques that are designed especially to raise them.

Before we introduce practical strategies, let's delve into the minds of our children and see the world from their perspective. By putting ourselves in their shoes, we can better understand their experiences and discover how to make things easier for them.

What Does it Mean to be a Highly Sensitive Child?

A child who feels everything around them with exquisite sensitivity, from the soft whispers of the wind to the gentle hues of a sunset, is a highly sensitive one. Such children have a heightened awareness of their surroundings, and their feelings are deeply affected by the energies swirling in the air. They may be the first to notice changes in noise levels, light, or even textures. Their reactions are often more pronounced than those of their peers, which is why they are often labeled as the "difficult ones" in the family and stigmatized by society. However, they are not "the problem," they are the ones "facing the problem." We need to offer them support, comfort, and guidance to help them deal with their struggles successfully.

Before Dr. Elaine Aron, the term "Highly Sensitive Child" was not even recognized by most psychology experts. This is why it was difficult to differentiate HSC kids from ADHD kids (attention deficit hyperactivity disorder) or Autism. However, Aron, a renowned psychologist and researcher, carried out extensive research in the 1990s, on the psychology and traits of such kids and clubbed them together under a single term "Highly Sensitive Children" or HSC. Due to her extensive work on highly sensitive people (HSPs), Dr. Aron identified that some children share this heightened sensitivity. Her groundbreaking research has shed light on the unique experiences of highly sensitive individuals which offers invaluable insights for parents like you.

Now, you might be wondering if being highly sensitive is the same as having conditions like autism or ADHD. While the symptoms of conditions often overlap with those of high sensitivity, they are not the same. High sensitivity is different from other psychological and behavioral conditions, and it must be treated as such. We know that Highly Sensitive Children are often deeply affected by sensory stimuli as they display heightened emotional responsiveness and empathy. They may become overwhelmed in stimulating environments but generally, they possess strong executive functioning skills and social abilities. In contrast, children with ADHD typically struggle with attention, impulsivity, and hyperactivity, so they often experience challenges with executive functioning, organization, and self-regulation. Autistic children are different in terms of social communication, sensory processing, and repetitive behaviors and they require support with understanding social cues and managing sensory sensitivities. So, although all three groups share some overlapping traits, such as sensitivity to stimuli, each presents its distinct patterns of behavior, requiring tailored interventions and an understanding of their unique needs.

Why Understanding Your Highly Sensitive Child is Important

It is said that understanding is a bridge that connects hearts and minds and paves the way for empathy, compassion, and genuine connection. Whether it is your Highly Sensitive Child or any other child for that matter, without completely understanding their psychology, behavior, and reactions to different stimuli you cannot figure out how to deal with their tantrums or sudden emotional outbursts. Better understanding opens up a way to good communication with your Highly Sensitive Child. When you know what triggers their sensitivity, you can adjust your communication style and techniques. You learn to speak their language which builds trust and strengthens your bond. Highly sensitive kids often need a bit more tender loving care to understand their emotions and sensory experiences. So, when you are clued into their sensitivity, you can provide the right kind of support – whether it is creating a calming environment at home or finding expert help when needed. And let's not forget about emotional regulation. These kids feel things deeply, which can be overwhelming at times. But when you understand their sensitivity, you can teach them cool tricks to manage those feelings and ride out the emotional rollercoaster with a bit more ease. Lastly, understanding your child's sensitivity makes you their biggest advocate. Whether it is talking to teachers or standing up for them in social situations, you have their back. And that is simply priceless!

Understanding Empathy

It is said that Highly Sensitive Children are next-level empaths! This means that to truly understand the psychology of HSCs and parent them effectively, we must delve deeply into how empathy functions. It is a multifaceted and often misunderstood psychological phenomenon that gives a person the ability to understand, share, and vicariously experience the thoughts, feelings, and perspectives of others. It plays a fundamental role in all our social interactions, communication, and forming meaningful connections with others. Even though we all are familiar with the concept of empathy to some extent, we know very little about how empathy develops in a young mind and what levels of empathy are there that are person manifests! There are three types of empathies:

1. Cognitive Empathy: Also known as perspective-taking or mentalizing, cognitive empathy gives you the capacity to understand and intellectually grasp the emotions, thoughts, and intentions of others. It allows you to imagine yourself in someone else's situation and see the world from another's perspective. Cognitive empathy helps you anticipate others' reactions and allows you to make accurate inferences about their mental states and adjust your behavior accordingly.

2. Emotional Empathy: It is also known as affective empathy or empathic concern. With this empathy, you share and resonate with the emotional experiences of others. When experiencing emotional empathy, you not only understand how someone else feels but also experience similar emotional responses yourself. This emotional resonance can lead to feelings of compassion,

sympathy, and a desire to alleviate others' suffering.

Research suggests that Highly Sensitive Children have enhanced emotional empathy. This is why they experience all the emotions so intensely and are more attuned to the emotional states of others. They may readily pick up on subtle emotional cues such as facial expressions or tone of voice and feel deeply affected by the emotions of people around them. Due to their heightened sensitivity, they have a greater awareness of others' needs and experiences. So, they are more compassionate and caring, always thinking about supporting and comforting others.

3. Compassionate Empathy: Lastly, we have compassionate empathy that combines the elements of both cognitive and emotional empathy. Through this empathy, you not only understand others' perspectives and share their emotions but also feel motivated to take compassionate action to help alleviate their distress or improve their well-being. Compassionate empathy includes both understanding and active engagement in supportive or prosocial behaviors.

Neurodevelopmental Basis of Human Empathy

Now the big question is, are highly sensitive kids born with enhanced levels of empathy? Or do they develop empathy because of the environment they are raised in? This "nature vs nurture" debate often arises when we study empathy in HSC. We can put this argument to rest by delving into the work of Jean Decety (2010) and other researchers in the field of neuroscience and psychology. Decety has worked to discover the neurodevelopmental basis of human empathy. To explore this phenomenon, he used functional magnetic resonance imaging (fMRI) to identify the parts of the brain that are associated with empathy. And this is what he discovered:

• When a person shows empathy, specific regions in the brain are activated such as the anterior insula, anterior cingulate cortex (ACC), and mirror neuron system. These regions are responsible for emotional processing, perspective-taking, and understanding others' mental states. This is why those with a high level of empathy can put themselves in other's shoes.

• The neural mechanisms related to empathy begin to develop early in life. This suggests that empathy is not solely a learned behavior but has a significant innate component. Even infants display basic forms of empathy, such as mimicry of facial expressions and emotional contagion and it proves that the foundations of empathy are present even in infants.

• The study also discovered that environmental factors such as parenting style, socialization, and cultural norms play their part in shaping empathetic responses. For instance, children raised in environments that promote prosocial behavior and empathy tend to exhibit higher levels of empathy compared to those raised in less nurturing environments.

The findings of Decety's research indicate that genetics and early neurodevelopment have a lot to do with empathy whereas environmental factors can further enhance the existing empathetic tendencies. So, HSCs are naturally born with enhanced levels of empathy because of their innate brain chemistry. That's why from a very early age they start exhibiting a greater level of awareness and consciousness toward their surroundings.

Elaine N. Aron, who was the pioneer of the term "Highly Sensitive Children," also deduced similar results after extensively studying the minds of highly sensitive individuals. According to her, Sensory-Processing Sensitivity (SPS) is a natural trait that is linked with deeper cognitive processing of sensory information, heightened emotional responsiveness, and increased sensitivity to environmental stimuli. According to her, there is a direct connection between SPS and emotionality.

Highly sensitive kids have high levels of SPS, so they experience emotions more intensely and they are more reactive to emotional stimuli in their environment. This heightened emotional responsiveness manifests itself in various ways, such as greater empathy, stronger emotional contagion, and increased susceptibility to stress and anxiety.

Characteristics of a Highly Sensitive Child

In light of the above-discussed studies, what do you infer? That Highly Sensitive Children have intense emotional reactions to stimuli because of their higher SPS? Well, that's true! However, there are several other traits that these kids have in common. Though they are directly or indirectly linked with SPS, it is important to explore all those characteristics before identifying your child as HSC.

Extreme Emotions

As we have already discussed, these children ride an emotional rollercoaster unlike any other. Their feelings are not just intense, they are downright extreme. This means that such a child may swing from ecstatic highs to fiery rages with very little middle ground. Parents often find themselves describing their Highly Sensitive Children as living life at the extremes, reacting intensely to situations that might seem minor to others.

The Meltdown Magnet

Highly Sensitive Children are more prone to sudden meltdowns. Their sensitivity means they get triggered by stress more quickly and that leads to more frequent and intense emotional outbursts.

Sensory Overload

It is not just emotions that run high for HSC, their sensitivity extends to their sensory input too. Bright lights, loud noises, strong smells - you name it, they feel it all. Have you ever thought about why your child freaks out over the flush of a public toilet or refuses to eat anything with a strong taste? It is all part of their heightened sensitivity which makes everyday sensations feel like a bombardment they can't quite handle.

The Constant Processor

Here is where it gets really interesting, HSC's brains are like supercomputers that never switch off. These kids are constant processors who analyze every little detail around them. They are the emotional detectives who pick up on subtle cues and changes in the environment that others might miss.

The Need for Control

Highly Sensitive Children crave control like a lifeline in a chaotic world. They develop fixed ideas and expectations about how things should be to cope with the intensity of their feelings and experiences. This often makes them inflexible and controlling, so they are unable to accept alternative ways of doing things.

The New Situation Dilemma

New situations? Yes, highly sensitive kids are not big fans of new settings. Their minds go into overdrive while analyzing every aspect of the unfamiliar environment and wondering what to expect. This deep thinking leads to anxiety and resistance to change.

The Frustration Factor

Highly Sensitive Children have a lower tolerance for change and challenges. That is why they often give up more easily when faced with a daunting task. Failure feels like a personal affront to them, and it triggers feelings of shame and inadequacy.

Perfectionism and the Fear of Losing

Derived from their fear of failure or losing, is their perfectionism. Highly sensitive kids cannot stand losing or making mistakes as they view them as a loss of control and a blow to their self-esteem. When they are unable to achieve their set standards of perfectionism, it causes intense frustration.

The Defensive Response

Now, when it comes to being corrected, highly sensitive kids are not open to criticism. It is their inability to handle change that makes them defensive in response to corrections. Even the gentlest of directions can feel like a personal attack and they trigger defensive responses like anger or avoidance in them. Moreover, they tend to be more self-conscious and easily slighted. They are hyper-aware of how others perceive them, so they take even the slightest criticism to heart.

The Science Behind Highly Sensitive Children

Through the research of Decety and Dr. Aron, we've gained some initial insights into the science behind HSCs. For a deeper understating, another pivotal study by Bianca P Acevedo in 2014 offers extensive findings that are worth exploring. Like Decety, Acevedo also studied the functional magnetic imaging of the brains of several participants. She recorded and compared the levels of sensory processing sensitivity (SPS). Her results showed that highly sensitive individuals exhibited increased activity in certain parts of the brain than those who had lower SPS scores. Brain parts like the insular and anterior cingulate cortex (ACC), which are linked to more awareness, showed heightened activity in highly sensitive participants. The insula in particular is responsible for interoceptive awareness (perception of internal bodily states including physiological sensations and emotions). Whereas ACC is responsible for monitoring and processing cognitive and emotional information, leading to higher self-awareness and regulation of attention.

Besides that, an increased brain activity in regions like the anterior insula and mirror neuron system (MNS), which are associated with empathy, was observed. The anterior insula is implicated in the experience and understanding of the emotions of others, while the MNS is involved in simulating and mirroring other's actions and emotions while facilitating empathy and social cognition. Additionally, heightened activity was also recorded in brain regions such as the medial prefrontal cortex (mPFC) and posterior cingulate cortex (PCC). The mPFC is involved in self-referential processing and perspective-taking, while the PCC plays a role in self-awareness and integrating information about yourself and others.

Without boring you with more heavy scientific explanations, let me summarize what these findings suggest. They simply explain the workings of the brains of highly sensitive individuals. They exhibit greater neural responsiveness to emotional and social stimuli due to the physiology of their brain. This leads to heightened awareness of internal and external cues, enhanced empathy and more pronounced self-other processing. So, the traits of HSCs discussed in the previous section are rooted in these neurological characteristics.

Genetic Factors Influencing Empathy

So far, we have established that higher emotional empathy in

Highly Sensitive Children primarily stems from their unique cognitive processes. But what role do genetic factors play in this? While studying the role of genetics, I discovered Varun Warrier's research. It sheds light on the genetic factors that influence empathy. His study suggests that variations in the LRRN1 gene, are associated with higher levels of cognitive empathy, which helps in understanding and interpreting others' thoughts and feelings. Another gene, NEGR1, is associated with emotional and affective empathy.

According to the results of his research, people who exhibit higher levels of empathy like HSC, tend to have such genetic variations. However, it is important to note that empathy is a complex trait influenced by multiple genes, along with environmental factors and the specific genetic contributions to empathy are likely to be highly polygenic (influenced by one or more genes).

Various studies have also found associations between variations in the oxytocin receptor gene (OXTR) and empathy-related traits. Oxytocin, which is the 'love hormone,' plays a crucial role in social bonding, trust, and empathy. Genetic variations in the OXTR gene are responsible for influencing individual differences in empathy by affecting oxytocin receptor function and signaling.

Put simply, genetic factors are indeed responsible for making a person more empathetic, responsive, receptive, and sensitive to their surroundings.

How to Recognize If Your Child is an HSC?

Are you still wondering whether your child is a highly sensitive one or is just like any other kid? I get it! It is difficult to recognize the symptoms and signs of high sensitivity in kids as most children tend to show some level of tantrums, emotional reactions, and anger at times. But, let me tell you that HSCs are unlike other kids, they are born with a higher level of emotional empathy, so they express and react differently to all situations. Here are some quick questions to assess your child's sensitivity levels. Recall all their past experiences and their reactions to different stimuli then answer the following:

Does your child seem particularly bothered by loud noises, bright lights, or strong smells?

☐ Yes   ☐ No

How does your child react to changes in their environment or routine?

☐ Yes   ☐ No

Do they prefer calm and quiet environments over busy or chaotic ones?

☐ Yes   ☐ No

Are they easily affected by the emotions of others, especially family members or close friends?

☐ Yes   ☐ No

Does your child seem to be more introverted or shy compared to other children?

☐ Yes   ☐ No

Are they particularly empathetic or compassionate towards others, especially those who are suffering?

☐ Yes ☐ Not much

Do they prefer spending time alone or in smaller groups rather than large social gatherings?

☐ Yes ☐ No

Is your child sensitive to physical sensations such as clothing textures, food textures, or temperature?

☐ Yes ☐ No

Do they have strong preferences or aversions to certain foods, textures, or sensations?

☐ Yes ☐ No

Do they react strongly to physical pain or discomfort?

☐ Yes ☐ No

Does your child have a rich inner world or imagination?

☐ Yes ☐ No

Are they particularly observant or perceptive of subtle details in their environment?

☐ Yes   ☐ No

Does your child become easily overwhelmed or overstimulated in busy or crowded environments?

☐ Yes   ☐ No

Are there specific triggers that consistently lead to overstimulation or stress reactions?

☐ Yes   ☐ No

If your answers to most of the above questions are yes, then your child is a highly sensitive one. Your little one now requires your support and guidance to steer through their own world of emotional sensitivity without getting overwhelmed, confused, and frustrated.

Fostering a Strong Parent-Child Relationship

"The relationship you have with your child shapes the structure and function of their brain." - Dr. Dan Siegel

In a world where every loud noise, change of environment, and bright light seems like chaos for a highly sensitive child, parents are the only refuge or place of solace that these kids seek to find comfort.

Your strong bond and relationship with your HSC take center

stage while offering them support and care. The more the child feels comforted by the parents, the easier their life gets while dealing with their inner sensitivities. There are various ways through which you can build a strong, deeper, and powerful connection with these kids, such as:

Emotion Coaching

Emotion coaching is all about recognizing, validating, and empathizing with your child's emotions. When you actively listen to them, reflect on what they are experiencing, and help them label and understand their emotions, this practice brings them comfort and they start trusting you more with their feelings. You can share personal stories of your own struggles and how you cope with them, to show them that it is fine to feel and express their feelings.

Create a Safe and Supportive Environment

These kids require a calm and nurturing environment where they feel safe to express themselves without fear of judgment or criticism, so offer them one. Create predictable routines and boundaries to help your child feel secure and reduce anxiety. Keep the communication open and maintain a non-judgmental attitude towards your child's thoughts and feelings to help them express their true selves.

Respect Their Sensory Needs

It is highly important to not only recognize but also respect your child's sensory sensitivities by minimizing exposure to overwhelming stimuli. Make your home sensory-friendly, for instance, you can go for noise-canceling headphones, soft lighting, or comfortable clothing, to help your child regulate their sensory experiences.

Encourage Independence and Autonomy

If you really want to see your HSC thrive, then provide them independence by encouraging them to make decisions and solve problems on their own. Offer support and guidance as needed, but allow your child the freedom to explore and learn from their experiences.

Celebrate Their Strengths and Accomplishments

Every step of the way, acknowledge and celebrate their strengths, talents, and accomplishments, to boost their self-esteem and confidence. Give them the opportunities to pursue their interests and passions and foster a sense of competence and mastery in them.

Making those simple yet powerful moves can bring you close to your kid, and you will become their confidant. This relationship of trust and open communication creates just the perfect atmosphere to raise and parent a highly sensitive kid.

Bottom Line

What have we learned so far? HSCs possess an exceptional ability to perceive and absorb the emotions and energies of others while demonstrating traits such as emotional sensitivity, empathy, and intuition. You can discern HSC by observing your child's responses to various stimuli and their level of empathy towards others. You can develop a strong parent-child relationship with your HSC by understanding and accepting their unique traits and needs, which can be achieved through creating a nurturing environment, validating their emotions, and teaching coping strategies. With that, we have reached the end of this chapter.

Now, let's move on to lesson one of HSC Parenting 101: Developing your child's emotional literacy. Let's begin!

Chapter 3

DEVELOPING YOUR HIGHLY SENSITIVE CHILD'S EMOTIONAL LITERACY

"Our emotions need to be as educated as our intellect. It is important to know how to feel, how to respond, and how to let life in so that it can touch you." - Jim Rohn

Let's imagine for a minute, you are attending a family function, and your Highly Sensitive Child turns to you and says, "I am feeling emotionally drained, frustrated, and upset because of all this crowd, I want to go home."

Life gets much easier when your kid is capable of identifying and sharing their emotions with you.

This ability to articulate their feelings can only be developed through emotional literacy. Feeling lost, confused, and unsure about their emotions, Highly Sensitive Children often exhibit their frustration in the form of emotional outbursts and extreme reactions. When they are taught to express what they feel and how to cope with it, most of their anger and frustration die down.

Early in my psychology counseling career, I met a young girl named Lily, who came to me with her parents. She struggled immensely with managing her emotions. She was highly sensitive and would often become overwhelmed by even minor frustrations, leading to emotional outbursts and meltdowns. She would frequently lash out at her peers and teachers, and it was evident that she felt misunderstood and unable to express herself effectively. Recognizing the urgency of the situation, I decided to focus on teaching Lily emotional literacy skills.

I started by introducing her to basic feeling words and emotions, using simple activities like drawing facial expressions or playing emotion charades. Over time, Lily began to develop a vocabulary for her feelings and that enabled her to identify and articulate her emotions more accurately. With this newfound understanding, she started to communicate her needs and concerns with greater clarity, both at home and at school. As Lily's emotional literacy skills grew, so did her ability to regulate her emotions. She learned techniques like deep breathing and positive self-talk to help calm herself down when she felt overwhelmed. Instead of reacting impulsively, Lily began to pause and think before responding and chose more constructive ways to express herself.

This transformation in Lily was remarkable. Her emotional outbursts became less frequent, and she became more adept at navigating social interactions and resolving conflicts peacefully. Lily's emotional literacy not only improved her own well-being but also strengthened her relationships with her peers and teachers. She became more empathetic and understanding for everyone around her. Her story highlights the profound impact that learning emotional literacy can have on a Highly Sensitive Child's life. So, by equipping them with the tools to understand, express, and regulate their emotions, we empower them to thrive emotionally and socially while laying the foundation for a happier and more fulfilling future.

Understanding Emotional Intelligence (EQ)

The power of regulating emotions effectively is broadly termed emotional intelligence. This form of intellect gives you the ability to understand and manage emotions. Through EQ you get to recognize your feelings and those of others, and with that understanding, you can guide your behavior and relationships in positive ways. Since Highly Sensitive Children experience difficulty dealing with their own intense emotions, they can benefit the most by developing strong EQ. According to Daniel Goleman's theory on EQ, emotional intelligence has five basic elements: empathy, effective communication or social skills, self-awareness, self-regulation, and motivation. Since HSCs are naturally empathetic, parents should focus on nurturing the remaining elements to foster emotionally intelligent children.

The Impact of EQ on HSCs

In 2012, Jeya Amantha Kumar and Balakrishnan Muniandy conducted a research study to explore the significance of EQ in reducing negative behaviors like aggression, which is particularly relevant for Highly Sensitive Children. Their research discovered that:

Emotion Regulation

With emotional intelligence in the equation, highly sensitive kids learn to regulate their emotions effectively and it helps them manage intense feelings of sensitivity, anxiety, or overwhelm, especially when they are surrounded by triggering stimuli. Research says that kids with higher levels of EQ are better equipped to regulate their emotions and cope with stressors. For HSC, developing strong emotion regulation skills can be especially beneficial in controlling and channeling their heightened sensitivity and managing emotional reactivity.

Empathy and Understanding

Since HSCs have this strong desire to connect with and support their peers and family members due to their innate emotional empathy, with enhanced EQ they learn to do the same without disrupting their own emotional and mental well-being. Studies have shown that those with higher EQ display greater empathy and perspective-taking abilities, so they tend to have more positive social interactions and relationships. Developing empathy through EQ can enhance the social skills of HSCs and foster deeper connections with others.

Conflict Resolution

Highly Sensitive Children often struggle with criticism and may find it challenging to handle conflicts and disagreements constructively. However, with well-developed emotional intelligence, they become apt at communicating effectively, unlocking all their problem-solving skills, and resolving conflicts like pros. Highly sensitive kids are more prone to internalizing conflicts due to their sensitivity, so they can develop conflict resolution skills through EQ to develop healthier interpersonal dynamics and reduce the likelihood of aggression or withdrawal.

Reducing Aggressive Behaviors

The study by Kumar and Muniandy also suggests that higher levels of EQ are associated with reduced aggression in individuals. EQ helps highly sensitive kids understand and regulate their emotions which leads to decreased impulsivity and aggression in response to conflicts. Simply, by enhancing emotional awareness, empathy, and communication skills, EQ interventions can help control various aggressive behaviors in HSCs and promote prosocial interactions.

Decoding Emotions

While playing with her four-year-old son Lucas, Sarah observed him struggling with a Lego puzzle. It seemed challenging for him to fit the pieces into their corresponding holes. Despite her offer to help, he adamantly refused and turned more agitated. As his frustration peaked, he screamed, tossed a puzzle piece across the room, and eventually hurled the entire puzzle in Sarah's direction. Does this situation sound familiar to you? If so, then your kid has to learn the art of decoding their emotions.

Children aren't born with the innate knowledge of how to manage their emotions; they must learn this skill. They gradually develop the ability to read, understand, and express emotions. This learning process is especially crucial for HSCs, who may become increasingly frustrated by their intense emotional experience due to a lack of understanding about how to handle these feelings. Let me introduce you to some effective strategies to help your child recognize and regulate their emotions:

Help Them Name the Emotions

Your kid must know what each emotion feels like, what is it called, and how it must be expressed, so they can communicate them easily. So, try to deliberately explain different emotions to them using various situations as examples. For instance, you could say, "Daddy went on a trip, and you are feeling sad because you miss him." By labeling emotions, you empower your child to develop a vocabulary for expressing their feelings. When you are teaching your kids, use simple language, pictures, books, or videos to help them grasp the concepts. You can point to a character's expression in a storybook and say, "Look at Little Red Riding Hood's face; she looks scared when she sees the wolf in her grandma's bed!" Here is a quick list of emotions that you can help them name and identify:

Emotion	When you are:
Happy	Feeling joyful and content
Sad	Feeling upset or down
Angry	Feeling mad or frustrated
Excited	Feeling enthusiastic or thrilled
Scared	Feeling afraid or fearful
Worried	Feeling anxious or concerned
Surprised	Feeling shocked or taken aback
Confused	Feeling uncertain or puzzled
Proud	Feeling a sense of accomplishment or pride
Embarrassed	Feeling self-conscious or awkward
Jealous	Feeling envious or resentful
Grateful	Feeling thankful or appreciative
Curious	Feeling interested or eager to learn
Bored	Feeling uninterested or lacking stimulation
Shy	Feeling timid or hesitant
Calm	Feeling peaceful or relaxed
Disappointed	Feeling let down or dissatisfied
Nervous	Feeling jittery or apprehensive
Silly	Feeling playful or goofy
Lonely	Feeling isolated or longing for companionship

Provide Them with Opportunities for Emotional Identification

Offer them plenty of chances to recognize emotions in themselves and others. You could say, "You are smiling while riding your bike. Are you feeling happy?" Or prompt your child to consider the feelings of others by asking questions like, "Joey bumped his head on the slide. How do you think Joey is feeling?" This practice enhances their emotional awareness.

Model Behavior

Show them what it looks like to feel a certain emotion. Start sharing your own experiences and feelings with your children and use them as teachable moments. For instance, you can say, "Do you remember yesterday when the bathtub wouldn't drain? Mommy got really frustrated. Can you remember how my face looked when I was frustrated? Can you make a frustrated face like Mommy's?" When you discuss your emotions openly with them, you help your children recognize and understand different feelings. You can use children's books to initiate discussions about feelings. During story time, ask questions like, "What is the character feeling? How do you know? Have you ever felt that way? What do you do when you feel that way?" Keep explanations simple, use visuals, and relate lessons to your child's experiences.

Coping Strategies

Let your children know how you cope with specific emotions. For example, you could say, "When I feel angry, I take a deep breath, count to three, and then think about the best way to handle the situation." By sharing your own coping mechanisms, you provide them with valuable tools for managing their own emotions. You can also ask your kid to come up with their own interesting ideas to deal with their feelings. You can use real-life examples or teachable moments, such as when your child is struggling with schoolwork and appears frustrated.

Lead By Example

You can share examples of how other family and friends handle their emotions. For instance, you might say, "You know what? Sometimes your grandpa gets really upset when things don't go well at work. What does he do? He takes some time to sit on the porch and think things through. When you feel angry, you can also take some time to think things over." This practice can help them understand that there are various acceptable ways to express and manage emotions.

Provide them with Alternative Strategies

While telling your kids what not to do, also provide them with positive and healthy alternative ways to express emotions. For instance, you can suggest they take deep breaths when frustrated, reach out to an adult for assistance to resolve conflicts, or ask for a hug when sad. Reinforce those positive behaviors by praising your child's attempts to articulate their feelings while emphasizing the importance of open communication and expressing emotions constructively.

You know what they say, "Practice makes perfect." The more opportunities you provide for them to discuss their feelings and practice coping strategies, the easier it will become for them to manage their emotions. Whether it is their playtime, car rides, or mealtime, engage them in conversations about emotions. This way they will quickly develop their emotional intelligence and effective expression skills.

While it is important to show your kids how to cope with emotional outbursts, teaching them new strategies during their emotional meltdowns is not effective. Only use the quiet and calm moments to introduce and rehearse these techniques. Let's say, your child is experiencing a meltdown because they want ice cream before dinner, they may not be receptive to practicing verbal expression of their frustration instead of throwing tantrums. In such instances, it is crucial to address their immediate emotions and reassure them with statements like, "I understand you want ice cream now, but we will have dinner in 5 minutes. You can have ice cream after dinner." However, once your child has calmed down, you can discuss the incident and explore healthier ways to express their emotions. You may say, "When you feel frustrated about not getting what you want, you can tell me without hitting or shouting at anyone. Remember earlier when you hit me because you wanted ice cream? Next time, try telling me how you feel, then take a deep breath to calm down if you are angry." This way your child will absorb and process this new information without dismissing it in pure anger and frustration.

Fun Ways to Learn Emotions

When it comes to kids, creativity sparks motivation to learn more. Fun games and interactive activities leave lasting impressions on their young and growing minds. So, use that knowledge to your advantage and try the following activities to teach them about emotions:

"Make a Face" Game

In your leisure time, sit with your kid and play this "make a facial expression" game. In this, you will make an expression and then ask your child to guess the corresponding emotion. You could say, "I'm going to make a face, guess what I am feeling by looking at my expression."

After your child guesses correctly, discuss what makes you feel that way and avoid complex adult circumstances. Then, switch roles and allow your child to make a face for you to guess. Be patient, as it may take time for your child to get creative with this game.

Share a Story in a New Way

Read a book to your child featuring characters experiencing various emotions and use different voices and facial expressions to communicate the feelings of the characters. Pause on pages where emotions are evident and ask your child questions like, "What do you think the character is feeling?" or "Why do you think they feel that way?" This will motivate them to discuss their personal experiences related to the emotions shared in the story.

Mirror Game

Here is another game that you can play with your child - the mirror game. You can either use a hand mirror or a wall mirror.

Take turns to look in the mirror, make an emotional face, and say, "Mirror! Mirror! What do I see?" Then, name the emotion, for example, "I see a happy Daddy looking at me." Invite your child to take a turn and say something like, "I see a happy Alex looking at me," while making a happy face. Let your child mimic the emotion you displayed.

Try mimicking 2-3 emotions per session.

Create an Emotion Book

Make a homemade emotion book with your kid. Use colored papers, crayons, markers, and a stapler to create a simple handbook. You can write one page per emotion or include multiple feelings on one page.

Ask your kid to fill its pages with drawings, pictures from magazines, or photographs that represent things that relate to emotions. If your child has a lot to express, let them dictate sentences about each emotion, which you can write in the book before they add their pictures.

Remember to do this activity together, as it is challenging for young children to do it alone.

You can add printed activity pages such as the following illustration to the Emotions book to help them write/draw about their feelings. The downloadable Companion Workbook will have a full page size of this illustration that you can print out.

Exploring my emotions

Can you name your emotions?
Write the names of these emotions.

_____ _____ _____ _____ _____

_____ _____ _____ _____ _____

Can you recognize your emotions?
Read and answer about you.

How do you feel when it is your birthday? _____

How do you feel when you fail a test? _____

How do you feel when it rains? _____

How do you feel when someone hugs you? _____

How do you feel when you have a nightmare? _____

Can you express and explain your emotions?
Think how you feel at this moment and draw it. Then explain why you feel this way.

[drawing box] _____

_____

_____

_____

While teaching kids about decoding emotions is essential, it is also imperative to provide them with different approaches to handling emotions every time they feel overwhelmed. Remind your child that while it's important to communicate their feelings, it's not acceptable to harm others or damage things.

Whenever they feel overwhelmed or overstimulated in a situation, teach them to:

• Ask for help

• Solve problems with words

• Use words to express feelings instead of actions

• Inform a grown-up

• Take deep breaths

• Describe feelings

• Consider alternative actions

• Relax and try again

• Walk away

• Request a hug from you

Activities

Other than games, there are several interactive activities that you can indulge your child in. Some age-appropriate activities that you could try, include:

Feelings Chart

This activity is perfect for kids aged 2-5 years.

For this, create a colorful poster or chart with various facial expressions representing different emotions (happy, sad, angry, scared, surprised, etc.). You can either create a handmade poster or print a template like the one given below from the Companion Workbook. Attach Velcro dots next to each emotion. Give your child pictures or cut-outs of themselves and family members then ask them to identify and match the facial expression that corresponds to how they or others are feeling. Use this chart as a visual aid during daily check-ins to help your kid recognize and express their emotions.

TODAY I FEEL

happy excited scared sad disgusted upset

sleepy annoyed proud worried silly exhausted

Feelings Diary

This activity is perfect for kids aged 6-9 years. You can provide your kid with a small notebook or journal and name it their "Feelings Diary."

Ask them to write or draw about their emotions each day, including what made them feel that way and how they responded. Set aside time to discuss their entries and explore healthy coping strategies for managing various emotions. You can help them identify patterns or triggers for certain emotions and brainstorm ways to address them effectively.

Emotional Mind Map

This activity is a little bit more complex, so if your kid is 10-13 years old then it's perfect to help them track their emotions.

In this activity, discuss different emotions and their

interconnectedness. Your child can use the pages in the Workbook, a large sheet of paper, or a digital mind-mapping app or tool. Ask them to create a mind map with any central emotion such as "anger," or "joy," then draw branches extending outward to factors that are related to that emotion such as triggers, physical sensations, and coping strategies. Let them include personal anecdotes or stories for each emotion to make the mind map more meaningful. Use this mind map as a reference during challenging moments to help your child understand their emotions and choose appropriate coping mechanisms. Here is one example to show your kid how to draw their own emotion map.

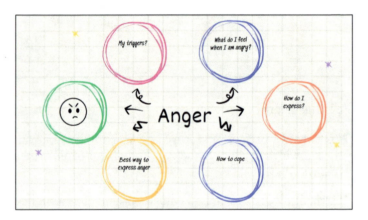

Setting Boundaries

One of the primary challenges that most HSCs have to deal with is overstimulation. Since HSCs are born empaths, they naturally absorb the energies and emotions of the people they interact with. The greater the interaction the higher the mental stimulation, which can leave them exhausted. This is why they need to know how to draw the line and avoid unnecessary interactions in daily life. Think of boundaries as protective bubbles shielding your highly sensitive kid from overwhelming emotions and allowing them to discern what feels safe and comfortable in their emotional landscape. Whether it is their personal space or privacy, they must be taught to protect it by cultivating a sense of self-respect and assertiveness. When kids learn to set their own boundaries, it helps foster mutual respect, trust, and clear communication.

How to Teach Your Child to Set Their Own Boundaries

Setting boundaries for HSCs is easier said than done. Their empathetic nature makes them more vulnerable and that is why I believe that they need to be taught to set healthy boundaries from a very young age. You can do this gradually by following these steps:

Start with Simple Examples

Begin by explaining to them that boundaries are like imaginary lines that define where one person's space or feelings begin and end. Use relatable examples that children can understand easily, such as not interrupting when someone is talking or asking permission before borrowing a friend's toy. You can also explain that they might like hugs from their family members but not from strangers.

Use Visual Aids

Instead of explaining the concept verbally, try writing it down or drawing it to let them understand. Visual aids can make this abstract concept more concrete for kids. Drawings, diagrams, or even physical demonstrations can help kids visualize the idea of boundaries. For instance, you can show the following diagram to tell them how much space and closeness they should share with those around them.

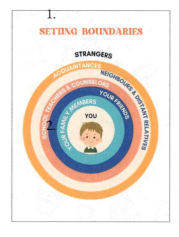

Family Members: Tell your kids that the ones closest to them are their family members. These are the people they can trust and rely on. They can interact with them daily.

Then comes their **close friends** with whom they can share their experiences and high fives. They can interact with them regularly as well (as long as those friends are not emotionally draining them).

3. With **school teachers and counselors**, kids can share their struggles regarding their studies without letting them enter their personal space. They should interact with them only in school-related matters.

4. With **neighbors and distant relatives**, they can play and spend some time occasionally at public gatherings and events. The interaction with them should be limited.

5. With **acquaintances**, they should only interact through handshakes and talking at a distance, that too on certain occasions.

6. Kids must keep **strangers** out of their personal space. They must only wave and smile if interacting with someone new. But make sure to tell them to keep a distance.

Respect Above All

Explain to your child that setting boundaries isn't rude or disrespectful; Instead, it shows respect for themselves and others by defining personal space. Emphasize that they should expect others to respect their boundaries and that they must do the same for their friends, siblings, and classmates. Even if they feel the need to step in and help others solve their problems, tell them to first ask the relevant person if they need their help or input. Getting permission to enter someone else's personal life is a gesture of respect and kids must expect the same from others while granting any space into their personal life.

Encourage Self-Awareness

When children are in sync with their feelings and preferences, they can easily say no to interactions that are not healthy for them. You can teach such self-awareness by asking questions like, "How do you feel when someone takes your toy without asking?" or "What would you like your friend to do when you feel upset?" This helps kids think and recognize when their boundaries are being crossed and empower them to speak up. If they feel the need to be left alone, or they are upset, then encourage them to communicate this need to their friends and other acquaintances.

Model Healthy Boundaries

Children learn by observing the behavior of adults and older peers around them, especially their parents. If you model healthy boundaries in your interactions by respecting your child's personal space, asking for consent before hugging or touching them, and setting boundaries with others in a respectful manner, they are more likely to do the same in similar situations.

Teach Assertive Communication

It is difficult to keep your boundaries strong if you are not assertive. Your kids must know when to firmly say NO to an offer to keep their personal space protected. So, show them what assertive communication looks like! It means expressing thoughts, feelings, and needs clearly and transparently. Teach them that they can use certain phrases to respectfully decline someone without being rude or feeling guilty about it. Show them how to use phrases like these when they don't feel comfortable doing anything or interacting with anyone:

"I'm not comfortable with that."

"I need my space right now."

"I would prefer if you didn't do that."

"Please respect my boundaries."

"I appreciate your offer, but I can't accept."

"It's important to me that you understand how I feel."

"I'm saying no because it's what's best for me."

"I'm standing up for myself because I deserve to be respected."

Role-Play Scenarios

Create imaginary scenarios that are relevant to your child's everyday life where boundaries might come into play. For example, role-play situations like sharing toys with siblings, asking for privacy when changing clothes, or saying no to unwanted physical contact.

Discuss Consent

As your child grows older, discuss the concept of consent in age-appropriate ways and very simple terms. Suppose you're introducing the concept of body consent. Start by explaining to your children that people outside of their immediate family should ask for their permission before hugging them, and it's okay for them to say no if they're uncomfortable. Show them how it is done by getting their permission before hugging each time. Your kid might ask several questions regarding this concept, so prepare well using the following answers:

What is consent?
Consent is when you give permission or say "yes" to others before doing something with someone else.

Why is consent important?
Consent is important because it helps you feel safe and respected. It shows care for each other's feelings and boundaries.

How do I ask for consent?
You can ask for consent by using words like "Can I?" or "Is it okay if...?" and wait for the other person to say "yes" before doing anything.

What do I do if someone says "no"?
If someone says "no," you stop right away and respect their decision. You can ask if they are okay or if there is anything else they need.

Can consent change?
Yes, consent can change. You might say "yes" at first but change your mind later. It is important to always listen and respect your feelings, even if it is different from before.

How do I show respect for someone's boundaries?
You can show respect for someone's boundaries by asking for permission before touching them, giving them space if they

need it and listening to their feelings and wishes.

Open Communication

Kids don't share their problems or everyday struggles unless they really trust you. So, you need to create a safe space where they feel comfortable talking about their feelings and experiences. Let them know that they can come to you with any questions or concerns about boundaries and validate their feelings when they express discomfort or assertiveness.

Reinforce Positive Behavior

When you see your child assert their boundaries effectively, appreciate them for reinforcing this behavior. Positive reinforcement helps reinforce the importance of setting boundaries and motivates the children to continue standing up for themselves in the future.

Kids don't learn overnight! It is a gradual process that takes time and repetition. Be patient with your child as they grasp the idea of boundaries and consent. Then consistently reinforce the principles of boundary-setting through ongoing discussions and practice scenarios to permanently gel this concept into their young minds.

Developing EQ in Your Highly Sensitive Child

All kids must learn emotional intelligence to understand and regulate their emotions, especially the HSCs. Their hypersensitivity makes it difficult for them to process all their emotions in a timely way and react accordingly. With emotional intelligence, they can fight this internal struggle and calm their minds when needed. As a parent, you have to guide them in the right direction to channel their emotions and this is where the following few techniques will help you:

Actively Listen to Them

One of the most effective ways you can promote and develop emotions in your kids is by practicing active listening. You need to give your full attention to your child's thoughts and feelings without judgment or interruption. By listening attentively and empathetically, you validate your child's emotions and show that they are valued and understood. Mavroveli & Sánchez-Ruiz (2011) found in their study that parents who actively listened to their children's emotional experiences tended to have children with higher levels of emotional intelligence. This suggests that attentive listening plays a significant role in EQ development.

Validate their Feelings

It is essential to validate your child's feelings by acknowledging and accepting them, even if you don't necessarily agree with them. This mere action of validation helps your kid feel understood and supported, which strengthens their emotional resilience and self-esteem. The same was found to be true in the study conducted by Mavroveli & Sánchez-Ruiz. It suggests that parents who validate their children's emotions contribute to the development of their emotional intelligence. When children feel that their feelings are acknowledged and respected, they are better equipped to understand and manage their emotions effectively.

Modeling Healthy Emotional Behavior

Mavroveli & Sánchez-Ruiz also found that parents who demonstrated positive emotional regulation techniques, such as problem-solving and effective communication, had children with higher levels of emotional intelligence. This highlights the importance of parental modeling in shaping the EQ development of kids. You are a role model for your children when it comes to emotional expression and regulation. When you model healthy emotional behaviors, such as expressing emotions calmly and constructively, you can teach your child how to manage their own emotions.

Appreciate their Emotional Expression

You have to create a supportive environment where children feel comfortable expressing a wide range of emotions. Even if they are sad, let them feel this emotion and understand it completely. Do not label any emotion as bad or good, let them know that it is natural to experience a wide range of emotions. Otherwise, kids learn to suppress certain emotions that are labeled as bad, such as aggression or sadness. You need to provide them the opportunities for expression through activities like journaling, art, or role-playing to help children develop emotional awareness and vocabulary.

Understanding Feelings Through Activities and Games

Kids learn through play! When they are taught through fun activities, they tend to remember those lessons for life. So, use your time with your kids and plan certain games and activities to enhance their emotional literacy. Here are certain ideas that you can try:

Tell a Story with Emotion Dolls or Puppets

This activity is perfect for kids between the ages of 2-5 years.

Use different dolls or puppets with different facial expressions to tell simple stories that illustrate various emotions such as happiness, sadness, anger, and fear. Start by introducing each emotion and its corresponding expression, then encourage them to identify and label the emotions displayed by the characters in the stories. You can also ask open-ended questions to engage them in discussions about how the characters are feeling and why. Keep your child indulged in this activity by asking them to act out the emotions using the dolls or puppets and let them explore and express their feelings safely and playfully.

Emotion Cards

Another great activity for kids of this age is to indulge them in a game of emotional charades. Create a set of emotion cards with pictures or drawings representing different emotions like happy, sad, angry, scared, etc. The following emotion cards are in the Companion Workbook. Stick them onto a piece of card and cut them out. Have your child pick a card and act out the emotion on it for you to guess. Then, switch roles and let your child guess the emotions you act out.

Role-Playing Games Focusing on Empathy

If your kids are 6-9 years old, then role-playing games are a perfect way to teach them about emotional regulation.

Instead of telling a story, you will be creating scenarios or scripts with them that would require children to take on different roles and perspectives, such as a conflict between friends or a challenging situation at school.

Ask your children to imagine how they would feel and react in each scenario, as well as how the other characters might feel. Guide them through discussions about empathy and emphasize the importance of understanding and considering others' feelings and perspectives. This activity helps children of this age develop empathy and perspective-taking abilities, which are essential components of emotional literacy and healthy social interactions.

Journaling Exercises

When your children reach the ages of 10-13, you can introduce them to journaling.

Gift them a journal in which they write all about their feelings and emotions. If they have no clue where to start, then you can provide them with prompts or simple questions to reflect on their experiences and write about them. Here are some good prompts to try:

> *How do I feel right now, and why do I think I feel this way?*
>
> *Can I think of a time when I felt really good about how I handled something? What happened, and how did it make me feel?*
>
> *Did I face any problems lately? How did I deal with them, and what did I learn?*

What makes me happy, sad, angry, or worried? How do I usually deal with these feelings?

How do I tell others how I'm feeling? Are there times when it's hard for me to talk about my feelings?

Did someone else's feelings ever affect me? What did I do, and could I have done anything differently?

Do I have any goals about how I want to feel? What can I do to reach those goals?

Are there any feelings or situations that I find tough? How can I get help or find ways to handle them?

What activities or hobbies help me feel better when I'm stressed?

How can I be kind and understanding to others? Is there anything I can do to be nicer to people?

Encourage your children to explore their thoughts and feelings about their behavior and relationships with others. Alternatively, you can ask them to write letters from different perspectives, such as a letter to a friend, expressing their emotions from their viewpoint.

Let your creativity fly high while indulging your kids in such exercises or activities. Figure out the interests of your kid and then plan an interactive learning session around their likes and dislikes. The goal is to introduce them to their own emotions and help channel them.

And that brings us to the end of this chapter. Here, we have explored the importance of emotional awareness, regulation, and expression in helping HSCs navigate their unique sensitivities and thrive in various environments. By fostering emotional literacy, you can provide your children with valuable tools for understanding and managing their emotions, building healthy relationships, and coping with the challenges of daily life. It is imperative to continue nurturing emotional literacy as your child grows, adapt new strategies, and offer support tailored to their evolving and ever-changing needs and experiences.

Chapter 4

THE ENERGY-SAVVY PARENT

"Our emotional energy is a key source of abundant energy that will help us fight uncertain and abrupt challenges which the future will unfold with every passing moment." - Sukant Ratnakar, Quantraz

Emotional energy is indeed a vital resource and Highly Sensitive Children tend to lose it every time they face an overstimulating situation or interaction. Such sensory overload takes a great toll on their mind, leaving them emotionally drained and exhausted.

This is where your role as a parent comes in! You have to be an energy savior for them. They need to learn how to protect their energy and it's only you who can model various energy management techniques to help them learn and adapt quickly.

A good friend's daughter is a Highly Sensitive Child. Emily would regularly experience emotional drain during their often rambunctious family gatherings. One time, I had been invited to join them when celebrating a holiday with a big family dinner, filled with laughter, chatter, and excitement. While everyone else seemed to be enjoying themselves, Emily looked highly overwhelmed as the evening went on. The noise from multiple conversations, the bright lights, and the constant movement around her seemed to weigh heavily on her sensitive mind. Eventually, she became withdrawn, her energy visibly depleted and she sat down in a quiet corner of the room. Seeing her struggle, I gently approached her and suggested we take a short walk outside to get some fresh air and space away from the noise. As we stepped outside, Emily's tense shoulders relaxed and she took a deep breath, I could see that she was relieved to escape that sensory overload.

By proactively managing their energy levels and avoiding energy-draining interactions, highly sensitive kids can relax and enjoy a balance of emotions, resilience, and stability in their daily lives. They just require a little support and guidance in this regard and that is what we will be exploring in this chapter.

Emotional Drain in HSCs

Highly Sensitive Children are emotional sponges who absorb every sight, sound, and feeling around them. Their heightened sensitivity lets them experience the world in vivid detail but also leaves them vulnerable to emotional drain.

Take the example of a bustling birthday party for instance, with loud music, flashing lights, and a crowd of excited kids. For HSCs, this environment can quickly become overwhelming, causing exhaustion and emotional fatigue. Their emotional battery runs low, and they need to recharge.

This is why it is important to understand how HSCs experience emotional drain, what causes it, and how to help them conserve their emotional energy so that they can enjoy all their experiences.

Energy Vampires

You know those moments when your child looks completely drained, even though they haven't been physically active? It might be because they have come across "energy vampires." These can be people, situations, or even environments that quickly suck the emotional energy right out of them. For instance, noisy and chaotic family gatherings can act as energy vampires for HSCs, leaving them feeling incredibly drained.

Even the negative vibes in the air can be draining for HSCs. Negativity and conflicts are two other forms of emotional vampires that affect these kids. Let's not forget that highly sensitive kids thrive in environments where they feel safe and respected, but energy vampires often disregard their boundaries. Whether it is someone invading their personal space or ignoring their need for quiet time, it can leave them feeling stressed and anxious.

All of this emotional exhaustion can take a huge toll on their well-being. They might become more irritable, withdrawn, or struggle with self-doubt and low self-esteem.

But the good news is that as parents, you have the power to help protect your child from these energy vampires. You can create a nurturing environment that respects their boundaries, acknowledges their feelings, and provides support when they need it.

Ways to Help Your Child Identify Energy Vampires

Do you notice your Highly Sensitive Child feeling exhausted after certain interactions or activities? It is vital to acknowledge the impact of energy vampires on our children's minds. You can guide your child to recognize these energy vampires and help them protect their sensitive nature and maintain their emotional stability.

Here is what you can do:

Define Energy Vampires

Kids don't know what energy vampires are and how to detect them. So, start by explaining this concept to your child in simple terms. You can describe them as people or things that make us feel tired, sad, or upset after we spend time with them. Tell them that these vampires can be someone who always complains, bullies, or makes us feel bad about ourselves. Vampires are not just people, but also the activities like watching too much TV or playing video games for a long time.

Encourage your child to avoid things, activities, or people that make them feel low and drained.

Teach Emotional Awareness

Your child might be unable to distinguish between feeling emotionally drained and simply being upset about a recent event if they lack awareness of their own emotional state. It is therefore crucial for them to recognize the impact of interactions on their energy levels.

You must help your child become more aware of their own emotions by asking them to label and express how they feel. If they are too young to identify and express their feelings, consider using emotion cards or drawings to help them pinpoint and connect their experiences with their emotions.

Look for the Signs

Ask your child to look for the signs and identify if someone is causing an energy drain for them. Your child should pay attention to their body and emotions and notice any changes in mood or energy levels.

Here are seven signs to look for in energy vampires:

- After spending time with them, your child feels tired, exhausted, or emotionally drained.

- Someone who often complains, criticizes, or focuses on the bad things happening rather than the good.

- They thrive on drama and seem to always be involved in conflicts or gossip.

- They tend to only talk about themselves and their problems without showing interest in others' well-being.

- They may guilt-trip you or use emotional manipulation to get what they want.

- They ignore your personal space or boundaries and may constantly intrude on your time or emotions.

- They always seek attention and validation from others, making every interaction about them.

- Interactions with them leave you feeling mentally drained or overwhelmed

If you or your child observes those characteristics in anyone, keep a distance.

Practice Self-Care

Once your child learns to identify energy vampires, they must be taught how to protect themselves through self-care. Healthy self-care activities can replenish their drained energy quickly.

Spending time outdoors by taking a long walk, cycling or reading, painting, drawing, and playing sports are some of the self-care activities that boost their energy levels. Help them develop a routine that includes self-care activities they find most relaxing and rejuvenating.

How Do You Manage Interactions With Energy Vampires?

It is almost impossible to completely avoid facing energy vampires, as they can be your kid's close family relatives, or friends. So, cutting them off is not an option. However, your kid can minimize their interaction with them by learning a few smart tricks. They just have to politely assert their boundaries to keep those energy-sucking vampires at a distance.

Know When to Walk Away

Let your child know that it is okay to walk away from any interaction that makes them feel uncomfortable or leaves them feeling drained or upset, even if it means distancing themselves from certain people. Help them understand that their mental and emotional well-being is the most important thing by modeling the same behavior.

Role-Play

The best way to help them learn how to deal with energy vampires is through role-playing. You can act like an actual energy vampire and then ask your child to assert themselves and set boundaries in a safe environment.

Create fake scenarios where they encounter energy vampires and ask them to respond assertively while maintaining respect for themselves and others.

Use Friendly Language

You can teach your child how to communicate assertively and kindly.

The use of "I" statements is quite effective in expressing feelings and needs without blaming others.

For example, instead of saying, "You are always so negative," your child could say, "I feel happier when we talk about positive things."

They could say things like:

"I have to go finish my homework now, but maybe we can talk later."

"I'm feeling a bit tired right now, so I'm going to take some time to rest."

"I promised my mom I'd help her with something, so I need to go."

"I'm really enjoying playing with my toys right now. Maybe we can talk another time."

"I'm in the middle of reading this book, but I'd love to chat with you later."

"I think I need some time alone to relax. Maybe we can catch up tomorrow."

"I'm feeling a little overwhelmed today, so I'm going to take a break from talking for a while."

"I'm having fun playing with my friends right now, but maybe we can hang out another time."

This way your kid will be able to politely withdraw from an unhealthy interaction without offending anyone.

Encourage Positive Relationships

Your Highly Sensitive Child must have positive relationships in life, with people who uplift their energies and support them. So, ask them to spend more time with friends and family members who make them feel happy, energized, and valued.

Model those healthy relationships by surrounding yourself with positive influences as well.

Shielding Your Child from Emotional Drain

As parents, fostering a supportive environment and understanding your child's needs are crucial steps in helping them fight the challenges of their highly sensitive nature.

Create a Safe Space at Home

HSCs must be raised in a nurturing and supportive home environment to feel safe expressing their emotions. You can create a safe space by establishing an open line of communication where everyone feels comfortable sharing their thoughts and feelings without fear of judgment or criticism.

Set a specific area in the home as a safe space where children can go when they need time alone to process their emotions.

Stock this space with their favorite books, creative supplies, and beloved toys so they can recharge by engaging in their favorite activities.

Teach Self-Care Habits

Show them through actions that mental and emotional

well-being is equally important as physical health. They are all interconnected so your kids must adopt a holistic approach to enjoy a healthy lifestyle.

Getting enough sleep, eating nutritious foods, and engaging in regular physical activity, are a few basic self-care activities that kids should focus on.

Emotional Regulation Techniques

Helping kids learn to regulate their emotions is a must for their overall emotional resilience. Teach them age-appropriate techniques for managing overwhelming emotions, such as deep breathing exercises, counting to ten, or using visualization techniques (which we will be discussing later). Let them express their emotions through creative outlets like drawing, journaling, or storytelling.

Help your children identify their triggers and develop coping strategies to deal with difficult situations, such as taking a break, asking for help, or using positive self-talk.

Build Resilience

Resilience is the ability to bounce back from adversity and it is a skill that parents can help cultivate in their children.

Let your children see challenges as opportunities for growth and learning rather than obstacles to overcome.

Teach them problem-solving skills and help them develop a positive outlook on life.

Strategies and Techniques for Managing Overwhelm

Do you ever feel helpless when you see your child becoming

overwhelmed and you're unsure how to help? Don't worry! There are some simple exercises that you can teach your child to practice with you and use whenever they feel overstimulated. By practicing these in their daily routine, they can manage their emotions and steer through challenging situations with greater ease and resilience.

Here are some strategies that many psychologists believe, can effectively control that feeling of overwhelm:

Cookie Breathing

This exercise is perfect for small children up to age 5, serving as an interesting introduction to mindfulness and deep breathing techniques.

In this exercise, help your child to imagine that they are holding a freshly baked cookie in their hands. Guide them to breathe in through their nose, as though they are smelling the delicious aroma of chocolate chips or vanilla. Then, as they breathe out, get them to think of blowing softly on the hot cookie to cool it down.

Guide your child to keep repeating this breathing exercise for 2-3 minutes to induce a sense of calmness.

Smell the Rose, Blow Out the Candle

This exercise helps young children engage their senses and learn the basics of deep breathing. It is ideal for children up to age 5, fostering an early understanding of mindfulness practices.

In this exercise, they have to imagine that they are holding a rose in one hand and a candle in the other. Inhale deeply through the nose, pretending to smell the sweet fragrance of the rose. Then, slowly exhale through the mouth as if they are blowing out the flame of the candle.

Hi-Five Breathing

Extend one hand with your palm facing up and place the index finger of your other hand at the base of your thumb. Trace your finger up to the top of your thumb as you inhale deeply. Then, trace your finger down the other side of your thumb to the bottom as you exhale through your mouth slowly. Repeat this process for each finger, inhaling as you trace up and exhaling as you trace down.

Through this exercise, kids can practice mindfulness and regulate their breathing in different settings. Show the 5 finger breathing illustration to your child, or have them mimic you as you go through it, to practice this exercise regularly.

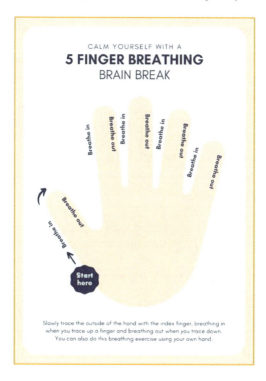

CALM YOURSELF WITH A
5 FINGER BREATHING
BRAIN BREAK

Breathe in / Breathe out / Breathe in / Breathe out / Breathe in / Breathe in / Breathe out

Breathe out
Breathe in

Start here

Slowly trace the outside of the hand with the index finger, breathing in when you trace up a finger and breathing out when you trace down. You can also do this breathing exercise using your own hand.

Belly Breathing

This exercise, also suitable for older children and teens, promotes deep diaphragmatic breathing and relaxation.

For younger children, encourage them to breathe in for three seconds, hold for 3 seconds, and out for three seconds, ensuring they don't feel overwhelmed or forced.

Place your hands on your belly and inhale slowly and deeply for four seconds, feeling your stomach expand as you breathe in. Hold your breath for seven seconds, then exhale slowly over eight seconds, allowing your stomach to contract as you release the air.

Five Senses

Throughout the day, take moments to pause and breathe deeply while engaging each of your senses: sight, hearing, touch, smell, and taste. Notice the sights around you, listen to the sounds, feel the textures, smell the scents, and even taste something if possible. his exercise encourages mindfulness and presence in the moment, helping children and adults alike appreciate the richness of their surroundings.

Balloon Breathing

In this exercise, visualize your belly as a balloon that inflates as you breathe in. As your child inhales deeply, they imagine the balloon filling up with air, expanding in their mind's eye. Then, as they exhale slowly, they visualize the balloon deflating, gradually releasing the air.

By connecting their breath to this visual image, they can focus on their breathing and promote a sense of calmness and relaxation.

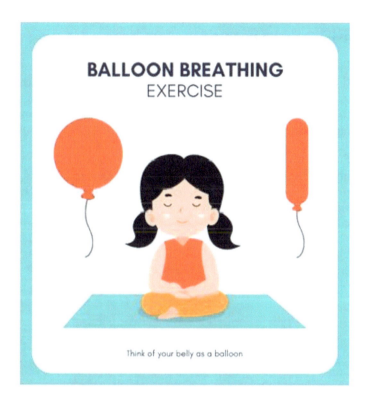

Think of your belly as a balloon

Grounding Techniques

For HSCs, grounding techniques are a secret weapon to instantly find calm and balance amidst the chaos of big emotions and sensory overload.

By teaching them these techniques, you will be giving your child the necessary tools they need to stay grounded and centered, no matter what challenges come their way.

Let's empower them to feel confident and in control of their feelings with ease and resilience.

5-4-3-2-1 Technique

Perfect for HSCs, this sensory grounding exercise refocuses their attention on themselves and takes their mind off the stimulating triggers. It engages their senses by prompting them to name specific things they can see, touch, hear, smell, and taste.

Every time they feel overwhelmed, ask them to observe five objects around them, touch four different textures, listen for three sounds in their environment, identify two smells nearby, and notice one taste in their mouth.

This exercise promotes a sense of presence in the moment by redirecting your child's focus away from overwhelming emotions or thoughts. Use this colorful illustration as a reminder and regularly practice this exercise with them.

CALMING STRATEGY

5 THINGS YOU CAN SEE

4 THINGS YOU CAN TOUCH

3 THINGS YOU CAN HEAR

2 THINGS YOU CAN SMELL

1 THING YOU CAN TASTE

Grounding Objects

Grounding objects are physical things that children can hold to help them feel anchored and secure when they are feeling overwhelmed - kind of like a security blanket. These objects can vary depending on the child's preferences and interests, but they often include things like their favorite toy, a smooth stone, or a stress ball. They can focus their attention on the sensory qualities of the object such as its texture, weight, or temperature.

Children can ground themselves in the present moment by holding something they are familiar with and creating a sense of safety and stability amidst difficult emotions or sensations.

Body Scan

This exercise guides children through a systematic exploration of their body, from head to toe, and helps them tune into physical sensations and release tension. Starting with their toes and moving upward, ask your kid to notice any sensations they feel in each body part, such as warmth, tension, or tingling. As they breathe deeply and intentionally relax each muscle group, they become more aware of their body and its connection to their emotions.

This practice is great for self-awareness and relaxation and that makes it an effective grounding technique for managing overwhelming feelings.

Imagery Exercises

Through these exercises, kids put their power of imagination to use, by visualizing mental images that bring feelings of safety, calmness, and well-being. For instance, if you see your kid getting upset or down at a party, you can ask them to close their eyes and imagine themselves in a peaceful natural setting such as their favorite beach or forest, and explore the sights, sounds, and sensations they experience there.

By engaging their active imagination and creating a vivid mental picture, HSCs can shift their focus away from overwhelming thoughts or emotions and find a sense of comfort and security in the imagery.

These exercises promote relaxation, emotional regulation, and positive coping skills.

Counting or Reciting

Counting or reciting is such a simple technique of distraction that helps children shift their attention away from overwhelming thoughts or emotions. For instance, you can ask your kid to count backward from 100 to 1 (or, if young, from the largest number they currently know), or recite their favorite nursery rhyme or song lyrics every time they feel overwhelmed.

When they focus on repetitive and rhythmic activity, it can create a sense of calm and stability in their mind, reduce stress, and promote relaxation.

This exercise works like a mental anchor for children to hold onto during challenging moments and regain a sense of control and equilibrium.

Progressive Muscle Relaxation

PMR is a relaxation technique in which you systematically tense and then relax different muscle groups in the body.

Kids can start by tensing their toes and then releasing the tension as they breathe deeply and slowly. They continue this process, moving upward through their legs, torso, arms, and neck, until they have relaxed their entire body.

Progressive muscle relaxation is great for releasing physical tension, reducing stress, and reclaiming a sense of calmness and relaxation in HSCs. By becoming more attuned to their body and its sensations, highly sensitive kids can develop greater self-awareness and emotional resilience.

Mindfulness and Meditation for Young HSCs

You know firsthand the ups and downs of helping your child navigate overwhelming emotions and sensations.

Well, guess what? Mindfulness is here to lend a helping hand! Mindfulness is a state of being in the moment. Some activities cultivate present-moment awareness and encourage HSCs to engage their senses fully. These activities can include mindful coloring, listening to calming music, or practicing yoga poses.

By focusing their attention on the present moment and letting go of judgment or distraction, they can develop a sense of peace and clarity amidst challenging emotions.

Mindfulness activities are perfect for promoting relaxation, emotional regulation, and resilience which makes them valuable tools for highly sensitive kids to cope with stress and overwhelm.

In a groundbreaking study by Zeidan et al. back in 2010, researchers looked into the incredible power of mindfulness in managing sensitivity. They found that mindfulness practices like deep breathing and body scan meditation can actually reduce pain intensity and unpleasantness.

So, why not introduce mindfulness to your little one? It is a great way for them to build resilience and cope with those tough emotions.

With mindfulness by their side, your Highly Sensitive Child can conquer anything that comes their way!

Simple Meditation Practices

Do you know that you can even teach your little ones some easy meditation exercises? That's right! Even at a young age, kids can practice meditation to keep themselves grounded and calm. It is all about finding simple techniques that work for them, like taking deep breaths or imagining themselves in a peaceful place.

By introducing these practices early on, you are setting them up for success in managing their emotions and staying centered, no matter what life throws their way. You will be surprised at how quickly your kid takes to meditation and how much it helps them process their big feelings with ease.

To teach them meditation, follow my lead!

Set the Scene: Kick things off by creating a serene and distraction-free environment. Find a cozy spot where you and your child can unwind without any interruptions.

Explain Meditation in Kid-Friendly Terms: Next, talk about meditation in a way that is easy for your little one to understand. Just tell them that it is a special time to chill out, relax, and tune into what's going on inside their head and heart.

Start with Quick Sessions: Keep those first meditation sessions short and sweet to match your kid's attention span - about 3-5 minutes long. Then gradually increase the timing as they get more comfortable with the practice.

Practice Breathing Tricks: The breathing exercises we discussed in the previous section can be used during meditation. Ask them to take slow, deep breaths in through their nose and out through their mouth. Show them how it is done and encourage them to follow your lead. Counting together can help keep them on track.

Dive into Imagination: Time to get creative! Guide your

child through fun visualizations or guided imagery exercises we discussed in the previous section. Think floating on fluffy clouds, exploring magical forests, or chilling on sunny beaches. Get those imaginations running wild!

Tune into Feelings: Let's turn our attention inward and use that body scan meditation. Help your child notice how different parts of their body feel, starting from their toes and working up to their head.

Listen Mindfully: Now, let's lend an ear to what's happening around us. Sit quietly and listen to all sorts of sounds, from chirping birds to the gentle breeze. Ask your child to soak it all in without any judgments or distractions.

Stay Patient and Cheerful: Remember, learning to meditate takes time, especially for little ones. Shower them with praise and encouragement, even if it feels tricky at first.

Add Some Fun: Let's sprinkle in some giggles and games to make meditation extra enjoyable. Bust out the toys, play calming tunes, or weave some storytelling into the mix. Anything to keep those smiles shining!

Last but not least, show them how it's done! Set the example by practicing meditation yourself. Kids learn best by watching grown-ups in action, so make it a regular part of your routine. You will be their mindfulness role model in no time!

Practical Exercises Designed for HSCs

Guess what? There are practical exercises designed specifically for Highly Sensitive Children that you can easily teach them with a little practice.

These exercises are supercharged tools to help your child deal with their big emotions and sensory experiences with confidence and ease. With a bit of practice, you will both be well-equipped to handle whatever life throws your way!

Journal Their Feelings

Journaling is a practice of having a private chat with yourself on paper! It is a way to organize and jot down your thoughts, feelings, and experiences.

For highly sensitive kids, journaling can be super helpful because it gives them a safe space to express themselves and process their emotions. Whether they are feeling happy, sad, or somewhere in between, putting pen to paper can help them make sense of what they are going through. They can write about their feelings or things they are grateful for in their journal:

Feelings Diary

This is the best way for HSCs to express and reflect on their emotions daily. Here is a simple illustration that you can share with your kids to write about their feelings.

By writing or drawing about what made them happy, worried, or sad, they develop self-awareness and emotional literacy.

Provide them with ideas and prompts to articulate their feelings and experiences healthily and constructively.

Gratitude Journal

In this practice, your child can write down three things they are grateful for each day. By shifting their focus to positive aspects of their life, they cultivate a sense of gratitude and appreciation.

This practice promotes optimism, resilience, and overall well-being by helping them recognize and savor the blessings in their life, no matter how small. Here is a great way to record their feelings of gratitude on paper or in a journal. Provide them with this worksheet to get started with the writing process, or use the Companion Workbook.

Mindfulness Activities

Any activity that your kid does during the day can be turned into a mindful one. The trick is just to stay present in the moment. The best part? These activities can be tailored to fit any age or lifestyle which makes them accessible and enjoyable for everyone!

Mindful Walks

You can even make your walks mindful by focusing on the present moment and engaging all your senses while walking. Take your child on a walk and ask them to pay attention to the sights, sounds, and sensations around them such as the colors of the leaves, the sounds of birds chirping, and the feeling of their feet on the ground.

Mindful Eating

Mealtimes can also be turned into a healthy session of mindfulness. Every time you eat at the table, ask your kid to slow down and savor each bite, and pay attention to the taste, texture, and smell without judgment. Bring their awareness to the eating experience. This can help develop a greater connection of food to their senses and cultivate healthier eating habits.

This practice encourages self-control and enjoyment of food and that results in a more balanced and satisfying relationship with cating.

Mindful Coloring

It is a great activity for younger kids (as well as older ones) who love to color. Every time you give a coloring book to your child, ask them to breathe in and out slowly as they color a drawing.

Let them feel their crayons or colors, and the texture of the paper and enjoy the experience without rushing them to finish coloring a drawing.

Creative Expression

Creative expression works like magic for highly sensitive kids! Most kids are not good with words and they find it difficult to write about their feelings. However, they are great at expressing their emotions through drawing and art. So, you can use this quality to their advantage.

For HSCs, creative expression is like a lifeline that helps them process their emotions, explore their thoughts, and express themselves safely and playfully. Whether they are painting a masterpiece, strumming a guitar, or acting out a story, creative expression gives them a chance to shine and show the world their unique perspective. So, why not encourage your little one to get creative?

It's a fantastic way for them to tap into their inner artist and let their imagination soar!

Art Therapy

Give them various art supplies and let your kid express their emotions through drawing, painting, or sculpting. Children can communicate and process their feelings in a nonverbal and symbolic way through their artwork. It offers them a safe outlet for exploring their inner feelings, thoughts, and experiences without the pressure of verbal communication. Such art activities stimulate creativity, boost self-esteem, and foster a sense of accomplishment as children see their ideas come to life on paper or canvas. It is also great for their brain development. Hang their finished art pieces in their room or anywhere in the house to appreciate them for their efforts and constantly boost their confidence.

Play The Play

Whether it is playing their favorite character from a story or reading lines of a play, role-playing offers a dynamic and interactive way to practice social skills, problem-solving, and emotional regulation. You can create different scenarios for them to act out. These scenarios can be about dealing with conflict, making friends, or expressing needs assertively.

Children can experiment with different responses and solutions in a safe and supportive environment. It can be a conversation between two friends, acting as a teacher or student, or playing other different roles.

This helps them develop empathy, perspective-taking, and effective communication skills.

No matter which activity you choose to engage your kid, the end goal is to make them feel grounded, safe, and relaxed. Every time they are triggered due to an emotional stimulant, these activities bring their attention back to the center and calm their nerves. That is the major aim of this chapter, to provide you with effective ways to teach your kids how to conserve their energy and replenish it through mindfulness and relaxation techniques. Here, I have highlighted essential strategies for managing energy as a Highly Sensitive Child.

This chapter also emphasized the significance of identifying and avoiding energy vampires, while providing practical techniques for staying grounded and balanced.

As you support your children on this journey, be kind and patient with yourself and your children. Whatever you teach them, first practice it yourself to become their true role model and a real-life example of healthy interactions.

Chapter 5

EXERCISE, SLEEP AND DIET

"When little people are overwhelmed by big emotions, it's our job to share our calm, not join their chaos." — L.R Knost

The importance of a good diet, an active lifestyle, and a healthy sleeping routine cannot be over-emphasized. Food and exercise work better than any medicine in the world. Together, these lifestyle changes can greatly help your kids deal with their sensitivities.

Having sugary and processed food, no physical activity and lack of sleep can greatly affect kids with high sensitivities. They can feel more agitated, without knowing how to channel their energy.

Luckily, you can change that for your kids by introducing healthy habits into their lifestyle. Let them learn through your example and see how good diet, exercise, and rest transform your lives.

Exercise

A systematic review was conducted by Janssen and Leblanc in 2010, which provided valuable insights regarding the health benefits of physical activity and fitness in school-aged children and youth. Their cardiovascular health significantly improves due to increased blood circulation, strengthening of heart muscles, and controlled blood pressure. Regular exercise leads to stronger muscles, and increased resilience, both physically and mentally. Physical activity is also good for weight management and bone health. From their growing mind to their muscles, bones, organs, and every part of the body benefits from exercise.

It is not just the physical benefits of exercise that make it a must-do for kids, but the emotional benefits are so wide-ranging that you can't even imagine. Research suggests that regular physical exercise triggers the release of endorphins, neurotransmitters that act as natural stress relievers, in the body. Now this is particularly good for highly sensitive kids, as this release of endorphins can help them stay relaxed even in stimulating environments. Plus, exercise also releases Gamma-Aminobutyric Acid (GABA) in the body, which is a neurotransmitter that helps calm the nervous system and regulate anxiety. Moreover, exercise stimulates the release of serotonin and dopamine, neurotransmitters that play key roles in mood regulation and anxiety reduction.

All this release of good and relaxing hormones can really help your kid manage their emotions. Plus, physical activity is a great way for them to release their energies and keep their mind distracted. As they engage in exercise and witness improvements in their physical fitness, strength, and abilities, children develop a sense of accomplishment and pride in their achievements. This positive reinforcement enhances their self-image and resilience which makes them better equipped to cope with stressors and challenges.

Suitable Exercises for HSCs

If you are wondering where to start, then here are some suitable exercises and sports that are particularly beneficial for Highly Sensitive Children. They will not only improve their physical health but also promote mental well-being:

Yoga

Yoga is an excellent exercise for highly sensitive kids as it focuses on mindfulness, deep breathing, and gentle movements. It can help them develop body awareness, flexibility, and strength while promoting relaxation and stress reduction.

The good thing about yoga is that you can pick and choose various poses according to the age of your kid. Keep these yoga sessions short and simple so that your child can focus easily. Even a 5-minute daily session would be enough for them to relax their mind a little.

Swimming

Can't get your kid to do yoga? Don't worry! Let them explore swimming. It is a low-impact exercise that provides a full-body workout while being gentle on the joints. It will improve their cardiovascular health, muscle strength, and endurance. Plus, it is also good for relaxation and stress relief.

The sensory experience of being in water can have a calming effect on Highly Sensitive Children which makes swimming a highly therapeutic activity for them.

Martial Arts

Karate, taekwondo, and judo offer various benefits for a highly sensitive kid, as they are good for their physical fitness, self-defense, and discipline. Martial arts training teaches self-control, respect, and focus, so think about just how valuable it can be for Highly Sensitive Children to develop emotional regulation and confidence.

The structured nature of martial arts classes provides a supportive environment for HSCs to learn and grow.

Dance

Dance is another amazing and mind-indulging activity that can give your kid a creative and expressive outlet for their emotions. Kids can join ballet, jazz, Zumba, or hip-hop classes to channel their emotions and energy.

Dance is good for the mind and the body. It improves their flexibility, coordination, and strength.

The rhythmic movements and music in dance can have a calming effect on HSCs and that lets them relax and release tension. Plus, dance classes provide them with opportunities for social interaction and building friendships healthily.

Tai Chi

Have you seen kids doing Tai Chi? It is a gentle form of exercise that combines slow, flowing movements with deep breathing and meditation. It helps them gain balance, flexibility, and relaxation.

Tai Chi is particularly beneficial for highly sensitive kids as it cultivates mindfulness, inner peace, and emotional resilience. The slow and deliberate nature of Tai Chi movements lets HSCs focus their attention, calm their mind, and effectively regulate their emotions.

There are several other engaging activities and sports that you can make your kids practice every day to keep their minds focused and grounded. From ice skating to skiing, cycling, archery, and skateboarding, let your kids explore their own interests and find the activities that best resonate with them.

Sleep

Living in today's hustle culture, we just don't realize the devastating effects of not having a proper night's sleep. A good night's sleep provides our minds with the necessary time to heal, recover, and rejuvenate.

Since HSCs' brains are highly perceptive and sensitive, sleep is even more important for them to recover from the daily triggers stimulating their minds.

Dr. Elaine N. Aron's research also sheds some light on the importance of sleep for highly sensitive individuals and highlights how insufficient sleep can exacerbate their sensitivity and affect their overall cognitive functioning.

For highly sensitive kids, good sleep is necessary to replenish their energy levels, reduce fatigue, and restore equilibrium. Insufficient sleep can leave them feeling overwhelmed, irritable, and emotionally dysregulated, and that makes it highly challenging for them to cope with daily stressors and demands.

Dr. Aron's research suggests that highly sensitive kids are more susceptible to the negative effects of sleep deprivation. Their emotional reactivity increases and their resilience decreases when they are exhausted.

Moreover, good sleep is also linked to enhanced optimal sensory processing and integration, particularly for Highly Sensitive Children. Without enough sleep, your highly sensitive kid may get easily overwhelmed by sensory input. It's not just that; when they sleep, their cognitive functioning also increases. Lastly, I cannot move on without highlighting the importance of sleep for their physical health.

Let's face it! The better the sleep, the healthier your kids will be.

Lack of Sleep and Emotional Sensitivity

Most highly sensitive kids indeed give their parents the hardest time when they try to put them to sleep, mainly because of their highly stimulated minds. It is not just a nuisance for the parents, but the struggle is real for them as well.

They need a calming environment, a fixed routine, and no stimulation to turn off their minds and go to sleep. When the conditions are not conducive, they may end up having little or improper sleep which leaves them emotionally drained, irritated, and highly reactive.

Sleep deprivation can worsen their sensitives and it may even interfere with coping mechanisms and self-care practices which initiates a cycle of emotional distress and sleep disruption in HSCs.

A Good Bedtime Routine

Knowing the harmful effects of sleep deprivation, you must be thinking: "What can I do as a parent to help my child sleep better?" Your concerns are legitimate and there is a lot that you can do to establish a good bedtime routine for them.

Start with Consistency

HSCs need routine and harmony in everything they do. So, regularity is a must while establishing their bedtime routine.

Don't let them stay up late even on weekends and holidays. Consistency is key to regulating the body's internal clock (the circadian rhythm) and it promotes better sleep quality for HSCs.

Choose a bedtime that lets them relax for the recommended amount of sleep for their age group. Most experts suggest that kids must take at least 8 hours of sleep every night to rejuvenate their minds.

A Calming Environment

Create a calming and soothing sleep environment for your kids and keep distractions away. The room they sleep in must have dim lights, and no noises and the bedroom temperature must be cool (research has shown that when the temperature of the atmosphere is lower than the body temperature, it induces better sleep). You can use blackout curtains, white noise machines, or calming essential oils to create a soothing atmosphere.

Relaxing Activity Before Bed

There are certain activities that are good at inducing sleep such as reading a book, taking a warm bath, deep breathing, gentle stretching, or listening to calming music.

Let your kid engage in those activities for 30-60 minutes before bedtime so their minds automatically switch to a relaxing state.

No Screen Time Before Bed

Exposure to screens whether it's smartphones, tablets, computers, or televisions before bedtime can really mess with their mind and disrupt their sleep cycle.

The blue light emitted by screens can interfere with the body's natural sleep-wake cycle and make it harder for your highly sensitive kids to fall asleep.

Let them engage in quiet, screen-free activities instead and set up a no-screen before-bed policy for everyone in the house and this must also include you! They learn by watching you, so sit by them and read stories and take deep breaths so they follow your footsteps.

Work on Any Sleep-Related Concerns

If your kid experiences any particular sleeping problem, then listen to those issues and help them. Difficulty falling asleep, frequent night awakenings, or nightmares, are some of the sleep-related concerns that most HSCs face and you can address these concerns promptly by seeking guidance from a pediatrician or sleep specialist if needed.

Nutrition and Diet

A good combination of healthy ingredients is everything that our mind and body need to stay fit and active. Diet has a special relation with emotional stability and sensitivity. A scientific study conducted in 20122, titled "A Prospective Study of Diet Quality and Mental Health in Adolescents," provided clear evidence that supported the link between diet quality and mental health. This study says that a healthy diet is responsible for better mental health outcomes in teens.

When Highly Sensitive Children receive adequate nutrition from a balanced diet, it can contribute to better emotional stability.

Food for HSCs

"Good Food, Good Mood," they say - and that's totally true! A balanced combination of organic and healthy ingredients indeed has the power to uplift our mood. Certain foods are particularly beneficial for HSCs because they are healthy and contain special nutrients responsible for inducing relaxation, calmness, and emotional stability.

Let me explain how:

Omega-3 Fatty Acids

Take Omega-3 fatty acids, for instance, they are essential fats that are good for brain health and mood regulation. Foods rich in omega-3, such as such as salmon, mackerel, and sardines are particularly loaded with EPA (eicosapentaenoic acid) and DHA (docosahcxacnoic acid).

The nutrients can help reduce inflammation in the brain and support the production of neurotransmitters that regulate mood. If you want to put your kids into a better mood then start giving them fatty fish at lunch or dinner, this will significantly enhance their emotional well-being.

Serotonin-Rich Foods

Serotonin is a neurotransmitter that not only regulates mood but also sleep and appetite. Some foods contain tryptophan, an amino acid responsible for triggering serotonin production in the mind. When your kids have a diet rich in tryptophan, this will counter their sensitivities. Tryptophan is found in a variety of ingredients such as bananas, oats, nuts and seeds (almonds, walnuts, and sunflower seeds), tofu, turkey, and dairy products like yogurt and cheese.

So, you can easily incorporate these foods into your kid's diet to support their serotonin production and promote feelings of happiness and relaxation.

Complex Carbohydrates

When compared to refined carbs, complex carbohydrates are good at stabilizing mood and producing serotonin. Whole grains, such as oats, brown rice, quinoa, and whole wheat bread, are excellent sources of complex carbohydrates. These foods provide a steady release of glucose into the bloodstream, so they regulate mood and energy levels throughout the day.

Refined carbs such as sugars and refined flour cause a glucose spike in the body as soon as they are consumed, so they are responsible for increased reactivity in the kids. Therefore, I would recommend you keep your Highly Sensitive Child away from refined carbs and introduce more complex carbs.

Dark Chocolate

Dark chocolate is not only a delicious treat, but it also contains compounds that can improve mood. It's loaded with flavonoids, antioxidants, and compounds like phenylethylamine (PEA) and theobromine, which have been linked to good mood and increased feelings of happiness and relaxation.

Try to get dark chocolate with a high cocoa content (70% or higher) and avoid milk chocolates that have more sugar and less cocoa. Give your kid a small piece of dark chocolate as an occasional treat to lift their spirits.

Probiotic-Rich Foods

Have you heard about the Gut-brain theory? It says that our gut biome works as the second brain which is responsible for producing emotion-regulating neurotransmitters in the body. Emerging research suggests a link between gut health and mood which means the healthier the gut the better the mood.

Probiotic-rich foods are particularly good at enhancing the gut microbiome. So, when you give your kids foods such as yogurt, kefir, sauerkraut, kimchi, and miso, the beneficial bacteria in them support their gut health and positively influence their mood.

Nature Therapy & Animal Companionship

> "*Nature is the purest portal to inner peace.*" - Angie Weiland-Crosby

Angie's words aptly describe the power of nature and what

it can do for us. From the colors of the sky to the blowing winds, chirping birds, the changing weather, flowers, trees, and mountains, everything is inherently designed to provide us with a serene home where each landscape can make us feel grounded. But the city life with its noise, artificial landscapes, and busy roads has caused a disconnect between us and nature which has negatively affected our mental, emotional, and spiritual well-being. The brain still craves that connection, and it does more so for highly sensitive kids because of the over-stimulation they experience all the time.

Spending time outdoors is highly therapeutic for sensitive kids as it gives them a grounding experience. Chawla's study about childhood nature connection and constructive hope also supports this claim.

This research has proven that nature offers a rich sensory environment that can help ground highly-sensitive kids and provide them with a sense of calm and stability. The sights, sounds, smells, textures, and colors of the natural world engage their senses and provide them with a soothing experience. It can reduce their stress levels, promote relaxation, and increase their feelings of happiness, awe, and interconnectedness. For HSCs, who often feel a deep affinity and empathy towards living beings and the environment, spending time outdoors allows them to foster a deeper connection with the natural world.

Now, I know what you must be thinking - "With all the daily commitments, studies, and extracurricular activities, how can I add spending time in nature to my kid's routine?" It is difficult but manageable. You just have to start by making little changes at a time.

Let me give you some ideas:

Morning Walks

Start their day with a short walk at a nearby park or nature trail before heading to school. Even 15-20 minutes can make a difference. If the school is within walking distance and you live in a nature-rich neighborhood then use the school journey for morning walks.

Weekend Nature Outings

You can always plan weekend trips to nature reserves, botanical gardens, or nearby forests where your child can immerse themselves in nature. Occasional camping trips are another great way to introduce your kids to nature.

Nature-Based Hobbies

There are hobbies like birdwatching, gardening, or photography that are easier to pursue, and they will allow your child to connect with nature in their free time.

Outdoor Study Sessions

If the weather is good, you can take them outside for homework or study sessions. It can be any peaceful place, like your backyard, a local park, or even a nearby café with outdoor seating.

Nature Breaks

You can add short nature breaks between their school, homework sessions, and other daily activities. For instance, you can take them outside to spend a few minutes observing birds or clouds during study breaks.

Let Them Have Pets

Pets can help them regulate their emotions and keep their reactivity and sensitivity in check. I know keeping a pet when you are raising kids can be difficult, but it is a great way to keep your HSC engaged in a healthy activity in which their high level of empathy is utilized in the right way.

The unconditional love and companionship pets provide can give them solace and emotional support. Playing with pets is also a great way to reduce stress and anxiety. Plus, kids learn responsibility by taking care of their pets.

Encourage Creativity

"The desire to create is one of the deepest yearnings of the human soul." - Dieter F. Uchtdorf

If you want your child to learn and explore both the external world and their inner selves, fostering creativity is key. Engaging in creative activities not only enhances their learning but also helps them manage their emotions without feeling overwhelmed.

Every child should have the opportunity to create and share their talent with their loved ones. It boosts their confidence and gives them the motivation to do more in life without doubting their capabilities.

Here are some easy and simple ways to help your kids tap into their natural creativity:

Painting or Drawing

Give your child art supplies and see the magic of creative

expression happening. Kids love to play with paints, brushes, and paper, and they enjoy expressing their emotions through visual art.

They can create abstract paintings, draw scenes from their imagination, or illustrate their feelings through color and form. Let them release their emotions through colors.

Writing or Journaling

Gift your child a cute-looking journal in which they can write down their thoughts, feelings, and experiences. They can write stories, and poems, or simply jot down their emotions as a form of self-expression and reflection. To show them how it's done, sit with them and write your thoughts so they can learn by example.

Music

Playing music is another healthy way to calm the mind and express emotions. Let your child explore the power of music. You can buy them their favorite instrument, and let them explore singing or composing their own songs.

Music is a powerful medium for emotional expression and can help highly sensitive kids connect with their feelings profoundly.

Drama or Role-Playing

Drama activities or role-playing games are another creative way for your children to express their emotions and channel their energies. Your children can act out different scenarios and characters with you or they can play with one another.

This can help them explore different emotions and perspectives playfully and interactively.

Crafts and DIY Projects

These projects are perfect to spark their creativity and to help them constructively use their energies. When they create something out of their own hands, it boosts their confidence and uplifts their mood. You can provide them with different materials to get started such as clay, beads, or recycled materials. They can create a gift for a friend, a home décor piece, pottery, or anything they feel like making.

With that, we have almost reached the end of this chapter. Here, we learned how important it is for your sensitive kid to get moving. Exercise is not just necessary for staying fit, but it helps them feel better emotionally too! We explored fun activities like yoga, going for walks, or playing with friends.

We also learned how eating healthy foods, like fruits and veggies, can make a big difference in how they feel. And let's not forget about sleep! Getting proper sleep is super important, so we explored some ways to create a cozy bedtime routine that will help your kids snooze better. And since spending time in nature or having a pet can also help your child feel happier and less stressed, we have discussed that as well.

Finally, we discovered some fun ways for your kids to express themselves through art, music, or writing.

Team up with your kids and be their support to gradually incorporate all those lifestyle changes to make their daily lives healthier and happier than ever.

Activities & Exercises

Are you thinking about different exercises to engage your kid? Try these simple yet really fun activities to spend some quality time with your kids and help them counter their sensitivities:

Plan An Outdoor Scavenger Hunt

Through this one activity, your kid will get to spend time in nature, use their critical thinking skills, and boost their self-esteem. Simply write a list of items found in nature (pinecone, butterfly, etc.) and go out on a scavenger hunt together in a local park.

DIY Smoothie Bar

One amazing way to introduce your kid to healthy ingredients while enhancing their kitchen skills is to set up a "make-your-own" smoothie station with a variety of fruits, yogurt, and healthy toppings. Then ask your child to create their own nutritious drink.

Bedtime Story Yoga

Before going to bed, sit with your kid in their room and practice gentle yoga poses with them. You can try child's pose, cat/cow stretch, and legs-up-the-wall pose to relax their mind and yours as well. You can find these poses on the internet, simply follow the given instructions and be careful to avoid overstretching.

Nature Therapy

Go on a stroll in a nearby park or garden with your kid and ask them to observe their surroundings and write about their observations in a nature journal. They can add different drawings, and descriptions or even paste the collected items like leaves or flowers into this journal.

Remember: you can download your bonus gift of the Companion Workbook & Journal, which supports the activities in this book.

Chapter 6

YOUR CHILD'S RELATIONSHIPS

"The more healthy relationships a child has, the more likely he will be to recover from trauma and thrive. Relationships are the agents of change and the most powerful therapy is human love." - Bruce D. Perry

Growing kids need our help and guidance to learn how to create healthy bonds while preserving their boundaries. Highly sensitive kids require even more assistance and support during this process as their empathetic nature, emotional sensitivity, and reactivity often pose great difficulty for them to maintain relationships while keeping their guards up.

Their heightened empathy makes them an easy target for energy vampires, so they need to learn how to deal with people and socialize with them without sacrificing their mental peace and sanity.

In this chapter, we will explore the importance of relationships in your child's life, and help them recognize and manage their sensory overload in social settings. This will enable them to foster healthy peer relations, regulate their emotions, and cultivate resilience in the face of social challenges.

Understanding Sibling Dynamics and Developing Harmonious Family Relationships

One of the very early relationships that your Highly Sensitive Child will create in their life is with their siblings. Children learn a great deal from sibling dynamics. They consciously or subconsciously compare themselves to their siblings and constantly observe your behavior in contrast to your attitude towards their brothers or sisters.

Plus, your indulgence in your highly sensitive kid can also affect the emotional and mental well-being of other offspring. So, when raising an HSC in a house with siblings, you will be treading a fine line. You will have to bring in a sense of balance and equilibrium to keep all your kids happy, healthy, and satisfied.

Tsao and Odom's study on sibling relationships involving individuals with autism spectrum disorders (ASD) also showed that having a neurodivergent sibling can impact the entire family. Similarly, in families with Highly Sensitive Children, sibling relationships require extra understanding and support. Studies say that siblings of HSCs often develop heightened empathy and compassion, as they learn to deal with their sibling's sensitivities and emotions. However, they may also face challenges, like feelings of frustration or resentment.

So, what can you do to manage this dynamic? Certain techniques can ease this process for you. Drawing from Dr. Elaine Aron's research on Highly Sensitive People (HSPs), it is essential to recognize and validate the unique needs of HSCs within the family context. Aron emphasizes the importance of creating a supportive environment where sensitivity is understood and respected.

So, here is what you can do:

Go With Open Communication

Whether it's your highly sensitive kid or their siblings, talk to them openly and listen to their concerns actively. You can even make them sit together and discuss the matters at hand to foster a relationship of trust and openness between them.

Divide Your Time and Attention Equally Among Kids

Just because your highly sensitive kid needs extra support and attention doesn't mean you must give all your time to them. Treat them like any other child to give them a sense of normality. When engaging your HSC in any activity, include your other children as well to maintain harmony and balance in the family.

Take Other Kids in Confidence

Siblings of HSCs must know about their heightened sensitivity and the challenges they face because of it. The better they understand the struggle of an HSC the easier it will be for them to accept their behavior and to deal with it from a position of care and empathy. So, sit with them and make them aware of the perks and perils of high sensitivity.

Demonstrate Acceptance and Promote Inclusion

Show them how you give respect to gain respect and display the power of mutual love and care. Let each of your kids enjoy their own space and don't force them to interact with one another when they just want a little time with themselves.

Fostering Harmonious Relationships

Highly sensitive kids face a variety of challenges when developing relationships with others, all because their heightened sensitivity to sensory stimuli can lead to feelings of overstimulation and anxiety in social settings. They can feel completely drained after interacting with others and their mental health takes a huge toll because of it. These kids also struggle to regulate their intense emotions and they absorb the emotions of others which leaves them emotionally exhausted.

It is difficult to establish boundaries for them and they also fear rejection or criticism which further complicates their social interactions with others. Misunderstandings by peers and a lack of social support can exacerbate their feelings of isolation and alienation, while self-identity problems related to their sensitivity may lower their self-esteem and confidence in social situations.

To navigate these challenges, your child needs to learn how to socialize while maintaining their boundaries. They must also learn to overcome their fears and not let arbitrary criticism impact their self-esteem. We've explored several techniques in previous chapters that can help these children develop social skills and form harmonious relationships with others.

Such methods include:

1. Emotional regulation through mindfulness and meditation to keep them calm and centered in any social setting.

2. Drawing healthy boundaries around them by learning to say no to others and understanding your limitations.

3. Boosting their self-confidence by working on DIY projects, and participating in sports and other creative

activities.

Besides those measures, you should constantly educate your peers about your child's challenges of high sensitivity to promote its acceptance. Plus, help your child find like-minded peers to interact with so that they can feel welcomed and more uplifted every time they interact with them.

Navigating Friendships

In her book, "The Empath's Survival Guide," Dr. Judith Orloff shared some practical tips for highly sensitive kids to deal with their friendships. Making new friends and communicating with existing friends is difficult for HSCs as they struggle with sensory overload and most social settings are nerve-wracking for them. They can't go to parties with loud music or noise, and they can't hang out with friends for long hours without feeling drained. They must know how much stimulation their mind can tolerate and respect their brain's innate needs by avoiding the triggers that burden their nerves. You can teach your child different ways to prevent such overstimulation or techniques to cope with them.

1. Let them know that setting boundaries doesn't make them a bad friend, it makes them a wise and smart person who knows when to step in and when to stay away from situations.

2. Ask them to regularly practice deep breathing and visualization exercises to cope and manage their sensory input for any social setting.

3. Instead of making your child avoid social interaction, teach them its importance and show them how positive communication takes place through open communication and active listening.

4. Introduce them to one-on-one conversations or small

group interactions with people they are comfortable with. Interacting in this limited setting will let your kid practice their social skills without feeling drained.

5. Confidence and authenticity are keys to good communication, so let them accept who they are and be confident in presenting their true authentic self to the world.

Navigating School

Highly sensitive kids face huge challenges in school settings due to several reasons. It's a place with lots of noise and activity. In a bustling classroom environment, the mix of auditory, visual, and tactile inputs can quickly become overwhelming for them which causes stress, anxiety, or even sensory overload. This is why most parents see their HSCs experience difficulty at school. Plus, the academic and peer pressure makes their school experience even more unbearable. The research conducted by Shimizu has also proven that kids with higher sensory processing abilities experience more attention-related issues during their academic endeavors. This underscores the importance of helping these kids manage their experiences and enjoy school life without letting it disrupt their emotional health. Here is what you can do:

1. Spread awareness among teachers and counselors so they can help establish an environment necessary for HSCs to focus on their studies. You can even advocate for creating a sensory-friendly classroom environment. This can include minimizing visual clutter, reducing auditory distractions through noise-canceling headphones or soft background music, and offering kids fidget tools or sensory-friendly seating options to help them stay focused and comfortable during lessons.

2. Teach your child the art of self-advocacy. There is nothing wrong in conveying their needs for boundaries and space. Your kid must know when and how to use this correctly with confidence.

3. Short breaks are a good way for your HSC to pause and recharge. In between classes they can take a walk outside, stretch, or meditate a little to relax and unwind their mind. They can listen to music or soothing sounds as well.

4. Completing school assignments and big projects may get quite overwhelming for HSCs, so should plan ahead of deadlines and divide tasks into smaller and manageable steps. For instance, if a big math test is coming up, ask them to study two hours a day for the next six days to complete the syllabus in time. With each milestone achieved, they will feel less stressed than before.

Building Self-Esteem

Self-esteem works like an armor for Highly Sensitive Children. We know that HSCs tend to soak up everything around them like a sponge, which means they can easily get knocked down by negative vibes or criticism. A healthy dose of self-esteem acts like a shield that helps them bounce back from tough stuff. It makes them feel good about who they are, helps them know their worth, and believes in themselves, even when things get rough. With a solid foundation of self-esteem, HSCs can take on the world with confidence and resilience.

Here are some ways you can nurture your child's self-esteem:

Affirmations

Ask your child to repeat daily positive affirmations, tailored to their unique qualities and strengths. Before going to school (or any other suitable time of the day), stand in front of the mirror with them and say affirmations like:

"I am strong, even when things feel overwhelming."

"My sensitivity is a superpower that helps me understand others deeply."

"I am enough, just as I am."

"I embrace my feelings and honor my emotions."

"I am surrounded by love and support."

"I am capable of handling whatever comes my way."

"My unique perspective adds value to the world."

"I trust myself to make good decisions."

"I deserve to take breaks and care for myself."

"I am proud of who I am, sensitive and all."

Repeat this practice daily for 2-3 minutes and you will see a new wave of energy running through your child. This will help them feel confident for the rest of the day.

Validate their feelings

Validate your kid's emotions and experiences. You have to acknowledge that their sensitivity is valid and worthy of respect. When you validate their feelings, you help them develop a sense of self-acceptance and confidence in expressing themselves authentically.

Encourage strengths

Help your child focus on their strengths and talents instead of their weaknesses. Celebrate their achievements and efforts with them, so they learn to cherish themselves for what they accomplished instead of regretting what they couldn't. Provide opportunities for them to explore their interests and passions, whether it is through creative activities, sports, or academic pursuits. By nurturing their strengths, you help them build their self-belief.

Foster their inner resilience

Teach your child coping skills and resilience-building strategies to deal with challenges and setbacks. Help them to acknowledge and accept their mistakes while learning from them. Let them know that setbacks are a natural part of learning and growth, and it is okay to move past them without letting the failures define who they are. Through this resilience, your child gains the confidence to overcome any obstacle and persevere in the face of adversity.

Set realistic expectations

Every kid is unique, and they all need freedom to grow according to their strengths and limitations. Unrealistic expectations put unnecessary pressure on them which hinders their growth. Despite all your efforts and input, you cannot expect any standard outcome. So, avoid comparing your kid to others, as this can undermine their self-confidence. Instead, appreciate their individuality and focus on encouraging their personal growth and progress at their own pace.

Lead by example

When you model positive self-esteem and self-care behaviors, your child emulates them. Show self-love, self-compassion, and self-acceptance through your words and actions, and let your kids see that it is okay to embrace your imperfections and celebrate your strengths. With your example, you can inspire your children to develop a healthy sense of self-esteem in themselves.

Create a supportive environment

Your child must feel safe, loved, and accepted in their home environment. Turn your house into a safe haven for your kids and practice open communication and active listening, so your child won't fear expressing their thoughts, feelings, and concerns.

Bullying and Peer Pressure

Heightened empath qualities make HSCs an easy target for bullies. They are naturally kind and caring, so being mean to others even when they are bullied is not in their DNA. However, they can be taught to stand up for themselves and not cave in under pressure. A research study on "Peer Victimization Among School-aged Children with Chronic Conditions" has also given us insights into how sensitive children can be more susceptible to bullying. While this study specifically focuses on children with ADHD, its findings are extrapolated to understand the vulnerabilities of HSCs in similar situations. HSCs may stand out from their peers due to their emotional responsiveness, empathy, and depth of feeling. Unfortunately, these traits can make them targets for bullying, as bullies may perceive sensitivity as a sign of weakness or vulnerability to exploit. Moreover, HSCs also struggle more than their peers to navigate social situations or assert boundaries which makes them easier targets for manipulation or mistreatment.

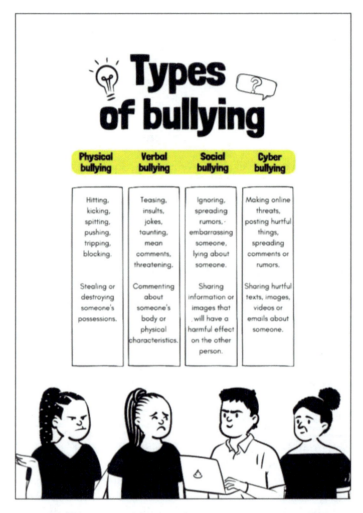

Types of bullying

Physical bullying	Verbal bullying	Social bullying	Cyber bullying
Hitting, kicking, spitting, pushing, tripping, blocking.	Teasing, insults, jokes, taunting, mean comments, threatening.	Ignoring, spreading rumors, embarrassing someone, lying about someone.	Making online threats, posting hurtful things, spreading comments or rumors.
Stealing or destroying someone's possessions.	Commenting about someone's body or physical characteristics.	Sharing information or images that will have a harmful effect on the other person.	Sharing hurtful texts, images, videos or emails about someone.

But that doesn't mean that HSCs can't do anything about it! They can also fight back the peer pressure and show bullies their place. They just need your guidance, support, and reassurance to handle it all like a pro. For that, you can implement several strategies:

1. Keep the line of communication open with them, ensuring they feel comfortable coming to you if they encounter any negative behavior in school or elsewhere. Ask them about their day-to-day experiences and provide them the opportunities to express themselves freely.

2. Provide them with basic awareness about bullying and how bullies must be avoided. The more they know the earlier they will recognize bullies and take action promptly. There are different types of bullying you can make them aware of. Here is a table that you can share with them to show how bullying looks:

3. Explain to them the difference between accidentally hurting someone with a thoughtless comment and repeatedly teasing others.

4. The confidence you instill in them also matters here! The best way to stop a bully is to show how strong and self-confident you are. They play with the insecurities and vulnerabilities of others. When you help your child embrace their imperfections and cherish who they are, no bully can get to their mind and sabotage their self-esteem.

5. If you suspect your child is being bullied, take proactive steps to address the situation. Communicate with teachers, school administrators, and other relevant authorities to make sure that appropriate measures are taken to protect your child and address the bullying behavior.

6. Ask your child to cultivate positive relationships with empathetic, understanding, supportive peers. Create opportunities for your child to socialize in safe and inclusive environments where they feel accepted and valued for who they are.

7. If your child experiences significant distress or trauma due to bullying, take them to a mental health professional who specializes in working with children and adolescents. Therapy can provide your child with effective coping strategies, emotional support, and a safe space to process their feelings.

In a nutshell, HSCs need all the love and support they can get from their parents, siblings, friends, and school environment. Together, you and others around your child can create a conducive atmosphere where your child can flourish without the fear of rejection, peer pressure, failure, or bullying. Teach them how to stay resilient and strong while creating healthy boundaries and maintaining positive relationships. To do so, you must constantly communicate with them. Your kid needs to know they can tell you everything without the fear of judgment. Teach them when to say "enough" and give them the confidence to stand up for themselves. Respect their need for chill time too, because too much noise and activity can really throw them off. Ask them to find friends who get where they are coming from, people who dig their vibe and share their interests. And remember, patience is a key here. Be there for them every step of the way, cheer them on, and celebrate their wins, big and small!

Activities & Exercises

Want to try some practical exercises and activities that you can do with your Highly Sensitive Child to help them navigate relationships? Give these ideas a go!

Emotion Check-Ins

Set aside regular time to check in with your kid and talk about their emotions. Use a feelings chart or emotion cards to help them identify and express their feelings. Discuss how they are feeling and why and come up with coping strategies together.

Try Role-Playing

Act out different social scenarios with your child, like how to introduce themselves to a new friend or how to resolve a conflict with a sibling. Practice active listening, assertive communication style, and problem-solving skills in this safe and supportive environment.

Collaborative Projects

Work on collaborative projects or activities with your child like cooking a meal together, building a puzzle, or creating art. Focus on teamwork, communication, and cooperation then celebrate your joint accomplishments.

Family Meetings

Hold regular family meetings where everyone shares their thoughts, feelings, and concerns in a respectful and supportive setting. Use this time to discuss family dynamics, resolve conflicts, and strengthen bonds.

Chapter 7

RAISING A HIGHLY SENSITIVE CHILD IN THE DIGITAL AGE

"Empathic children can teach us about compassion, kindness, and the importance of feeling." - Unknown

In today's technologically driven society, kids are exposed to a constant stream of digital stimuli. From social media to online gaming and digital devices, exposure to the digital world is mentally draining.

For sensitive children, who are already sensitive to all sorts of sensory inputs and emotional stimuli, living in this digital landscape is highly overwhelming and overstimulating. The fast-paced nature of digital interactions exacerbates their anxiety, stress and social pressure. HSCs struggle to find a balance and maintain their emotional well-being amidst all this. Plus, the prevalence of cyberbullying and online negativity poses another great challenge for your sensitive children.

So, while it is necessary to limit their screen time and set some digital safety rules, it is also important to give your young ones a basic understanding of the digital world and how they can ensure their safety by being tech-savvy.

Understanding the Digital World

Digital media has become an integral part of our modern-day society. If anyone believes that they can keep their kids away from internet exposure, then they are just being delusional. The question is no longer about whether to allow your kids to use digital spaces, but rather how to equip them with the knowledge and understanding needed to become responsible digital citizens.

This involves teaching them how to protect their privacy and emotional well-being, while respecting the boundaries of others.

When we analyze the wide-ranging effects of social media on our lives, we can't help thinking about the immense social pressure it has brought on. Everyone is out in the race to compare themselves with others and mold or fold their true selves to fit into the popular online culture. This pressure to prove your worthiness over social media has brought more challenges for highly sensitive kids who are already fighting with other sensory stimuli.

The research study, "The impact of social media on children, adolescents, and families" (2011), conducted by Gwenn Schurgin O'Keeffe and Kathleen Clarke-Pearson highlights the similar effects of digital media on kids and teens. The study also suggests parents, counselors and guardians take on the responsibility of educating children about how to create boundaries in the virtual world.

The Challenges for HSCs in the Digital Age

At a recent conference, I had the opportunity to meet Susan, a highly sensitive kid, who shared her struggles of feeling overstimulated and drained after participating in online gaming sessions with her friends. The fast-paced nature of the games and the constant sensory input left her feeling frazzled and quite exhausted. This overstimulation affected her ability to focus on her schoolwork and engage in offline activities. She was losing her balance altogether.

This digital era brings forth more mental well-being challenges than ever before and highly sensitive kids receive the greatest brunt of it. There are many different ways in which exposure to various online activities and content can leave an HSC completely drained and overstimulated. These include:

Sensory Overload

The digital world is full of bright screens, flashing images, loud sounds, and fast movements. For highly sensitive kids, this can be too much to handle. They can easily feel stressed and anxious because their senses are overloaded. Spending a lot of time in front of screens can make them feel even more uncomfortable and overwhelmed.

Emotional Intensity

Online interactions can be very emotional and intense. HSCs might feel a lot of pressure to fit in and get approval from others. They often feel strong emotions like loneliness, jealousy, and fear of missing out (FOMO) when they compare themselves to others online. This can be very exhausting for them because they naturally feel things more deeply.

Lack of Boundaries and Privacy

The line between public and private can get very blurry when kids step into an online space. This can be hard for HSCs, who need clear boundaries to feel safe. Constant messages and notifications can be overwhelming and that makes them feel exposed and uncomfortable. They might find it hard to set and keep healthy boundaries online, which can make them feel more vulnerable and anxious.

Social Media and Online Overwhelm

Social media and the vast amount of information online can be overwhelming for highly sensitive kids. There is so much content that it can be hard for them to process everything which leads to mental overload. The never-ending stream of updates and news can make your kid feel pressured to stay connected all the time, which can affect their mental and emotional health. This can stop them from taking the breaks they need to feel better.

Comparison Culture

Social media makes kids compare themselves to others. For HSCs, this can be very tough. When they see the perfect lives that others post online, it can make them feel inadequate and lower their self-esteem. In other words, constant comparison is the cause of emotional distress.

Dealing with Online Bullying

Highly sensitive kids are more likely to be affected by negative interactions online, like cyberbullying and harassment. Since they are so empathetic, bullying can hit them particularly hard. Negative experiences online can make them feel isolated, lower their self-esteem, and lead to depression and anxiety. The internet's anonymity and wide reach can make these negative experiences seem even worse and harder to escape from.

Research, such as Peter K Smith et al.'s study, also highlights the similar effects of cyberbullying in secondary school.

The question then becomes: How can we protect our kids from its negative influence? Some effective strategies include:

1. Create a Safe Space for Open Talks

Your kids must feel safe to talk about their online experiences without feeling judged. Start by creating an environment where your child feels comfortable to share their stories. Let them know that their feelings are valid and that you are there to support them no matter what. Simple phrases like, "You can always talk to me about anything" or "I'm here to listen" can reassure them that they can come to you anytime if they witness online harassment or cyberbullying.

2. Listen and Show You Care

When your child opens up about being bullied online, you must listen attentively. Don't interrupt or minimize their feelings. Show empathy by saying things like, "I can see how this is really upsetting for you" or "It must be hard to deal with this." When you validate their emotions, it helps them feel understood and supported. Avoid skipping straight to the solutions; sometimes, just listening can be incredibly comforting.

3. Keep a Record of Everything

Tell your child to save all evidence of the bullying. Whether they get abusive messages, screenshots, emails, or any other forms of communication from the bully, they need to keep a detailed record so that you can report the bullying to school authorities or the relevant online platform. Show your kids how to do this record keeping by doing it in front of them practically. It is also helpful to note the dates and times of these incidents to see a clear picture of the bullying pattern.

4. Don't Respond to the Bully

Ask your child not to respond to the bully. There is no point in engaging with the bully as it can sometimes escalate the situation and bring no positive outcomes. Instead, teach them how to block the bully on social media and other online platforms. Most platforms have features to block and report users. Explain to your child that ignoring the bully and not giving them a reaction is often the best way to handle such situations initially.

5. Teach Them Online Safety and Privacy

Your child should know that personal information must be kept private. Show them how to use privacy settings on social media to control who can see their posts and who can contact them. Explain why it is crucial not to share personal details like their address, phone number, or school online. Regularly review their privacy settings together to make sure they are secure.

6. Report the Bullying

If your child experiences any bullying activity online, help them report it to the relevant platform or website. Each social media site and online service has its own process for reporting harassment. Guide your child through the steps and show them how to fill out the report forms and attach evidence. This way the account of the bully will get suspended or banned, which is the best way to discourage such behavior.

7. Talk to School Officials

If cyberbullying is carried out by their schoolmates, then it is important to inform the school. Many schools have anti-bullying policies and can take action to address the issue.

Schedule a meeting with your child's teacher, counselor, or principal to discuss what has been happening. Bring any evidence you have collected and explain the impact the bullying has had on your child. Schools have to offer additional support and monitor interactions closely.

8. Boost Your Child's Confidence

In most cases, children hesitate to share their experiences and report them because of their low confidence. That is why it is your responsibility to boost their self-esteem and make them feel important. Help your child engage in activities that they enjoy and are good at. This can boost their morale and give them a sense of empowerment to raise their voice against bullying.

9. Keep an Eye on Their Online Activity

While respecting their privacy, try to monitor your child's online activities. This doesn't mean reading every message, but rather having an idea of what platforms they are using and who they are interacting with. Look out for changes in their behavior that might indicate they are being bullied, such as becoming withdrawn, anxious, or upset after using their devices.

10. Use Parental Controls

There are several parental controls that different software and applications provide to help monitor and limit your child's online interactions, try to use these tools to filter content, set time limits, and track online activity. They provide an additional layer of security and help protect your child from encountering harmful content and individuals.

Balancing Digital Life with Real-world Experiences

My 8-year-old niece is also a highly sensitive kid. She's sweet, imaginative, and incredibly perceptive. However, like many kids of her age, she is also drawn to screens and digital devices. She used to spend hours immersed in games and videos online. But as her aunt, I started noticing that this digital experience was affecting her in ways that worried me to the core. She used to become easily overstimulated, sometimes even feeling anxious or upset after spending too much time online. Seeing her struggle, I knew we needed to find a way to help her strike a better balance between her digital life and real-world experiences.

Now, how can you strike such a balance when we are living in this digital landscape, where screens seem to be everywhere? It is a valid question and one that many parents and caregivers grapple with. The key lies in finding creative ways to add both digital and real-life activities into your child's routine.

A study named "Parental Mediation of Children's Internet Use in Different European Countries," conducted by Sonia Livingstone et al. (2014) also claims the same. It offers valuable insights into the role of parents in guiding and supervising their children's online activities across various European countries. The study examined how parents can mediate their children's internet use, by setting rules, monitoring online behavior, and engaging in discussions about online experiences. Through a comparative analysis of parental mediation practices in different cultural contexts, the research sheds light on the diverse approaches taken by parents to manage their children's digital lives.

These include:

1. Being a Positive Role Model

Lead the way by showing your child how to balance screen time with real-life experiences. Make a point of putting away your own devices during family time and engaging in activities that don't involve screens. When you strike such a balance, you teach your child the importance of minimizing screen time.

2. Explore the Great Outdoors with them

The more you engage your kid in outdoor activities, the less time they get to spend online. Take them outside more often and enjoy the wonders of nature. Plan fun outdoor adventures like hiking, biking, or exploring local parks every once in a while. During school days you can take them to a park in the evening to indulge them in healthy physical activities. These quick outdoor adventures let your child connect with nature and engage their senses in a way that screens simply can't replicate.

3. Enforce Healthy Screen Time Guidelines

You need to establish clear guidelines for screen time and make your kids stick to them consistently. Set specific times when screens are allowed and when they are off-limits. Such as 1-2 hours of screen time after doing their homework. You can use tools like parental controls to help enforce these rules. If you follow these same rules in front of your kids, they will learn their importance and follow them without showing much resistance.

4. Nurture their Inner Creativity Through Hands-On Activities

Creative activities are super healthy for the growing mind of a child. They need to explore their creative side through hands-on activities like painting, building, or crafting. Provide them with materials and let them use their imagination to create something unique. These activities not only stimulate their creativity but also help your child develop problem-solving skills and build confidence in their abilities.

5. Giving Back to the Community

Besides outdoor sports and creative activities, there are other great options that benefit both the community and your child. Get involved in volunteering activities as a family and show your child the importance of giving back to others. It is particularly helpful for HSCs because this way they learn to put their empathy to the right use. Whether it is helping out at a local soup kitchen, participating in a beach clean-up, or volunteering at an animal shelter, these experiences teach them valuable lessons about empathy, compassion, and social responsibility.

Your active role in in shaping your child's understanding of digital spaces and tools can make a significant difference. It is not going to be easy for your highly sensitive kid to step into the virtual world. The online experiences are going to be super draining for them.

However, with your help and guidance, they learn to set boundaries, deal with bullies and avoid overstimulation. You just need to constantly model healthy online behaviors in front of them, keep the communication channels open, and allow them to freely express their opinions in the house.

Chapter 8

SUPPORTING YOUR TEENAGE HSC

"Sensitive children have an innate ability to understand others. Guide them to use this gift wisely." - Unknown

When your Highly Sensitive Child steps into their teenage years, the transition can be highly intense.

As they begin to steer through the complex world of adolescence, their heightened sensitivity can amplify the emotional rollercoaster typical of this stage. They feel overwhelmed by the increased academic pressures, social dynamics, and the sudden surge of new emotions and experiences. They might find themselves more affected by peer pressure, social comparisons, and the desire to fit in. This is the time they need your unwavering support, understanding, and a safe space to express their feelings.

Their sensitivity is a strength that needs to be nurtured with great care. In this chapter, we will dive into the experiences and challenges of highly sensitive teens and figure out ways to help them during this difficult phase of their lives.

Heightened Sensitivities in Teenagers

During the teenage years, kids become even more sensitive because of the changes in their bodies, social pressures, and figuring out who they are. Hormones like estrogen and testosterone increase which affects their moods and emotions and makes them feel things more strongly. They also care more about what their friends think and want to fit in. As they develop their identity, they become more aware of themselves and sensitive to criticism or rejection. They can become highly sensitive due to the following reasons:

Hormonal Changes

This is when hormonal changes play a significant role in shaping emotions and sensitivities. The surge in hormones like estrogen and testosterone in girls and boys respectively, can lead to heightened emotional responses and increased sensitivity to environmental stimuli. These hormonal fluctuations influence the development of the brain's limbic system, which mainly controls emotions and behaviors. As a result, highly sensitive kids experience more mood swings, impulsivity, and heightened reactivity during this period of growth and development.

In the study, "Adolescent Brain Development and Depression: A Case for the Importance of Connectivity of the Anterior Cingulate Cortex" by Erin Fallucca, M.D. from the University of Michigan, researchers examined the anterior cingulate cortex (ACC), a region of the brain responsible for emotional regulation and decision-making. The study showed how disruptions in the connectivity of the ACC during teenage years can contribute to mood disorders like depression. Teens with less efficient connectivity in the ACC may struggle even more while regulating their emotions and coping with stressors and that increases their vulnerability to mental health issues. Hence, they need outside interventions, support and guidance to cope with their teenage struggles. During this period of hormonal fluctuations, there are activities that your highly sensitive teen can incorporate into their daily lifestyle and keep their emotions regulated:

• **Mindfulness Activities:** Mindfulness is a powerful way to counter stress and overstimulation. It is a technique to ground yourself in the present moment. So, highly sensitive teens can benefit from mindful walking or mindful eating to regulate their emotions. These activities can reduce overthinking and anxiety, which are often heightened during hormonal fluctuations. To practice mindfulness, encourage your child to focus on the present moment during any activity. For example, if they are walking, ask them to notice their surroundings, observe the scenery, and feel the ground beneath their feet.

• **Regular Exercise & Routine Workouts:** Regular physical activities take the mind off stressful situations. Sports, dance, or yoga are all great ways to balance hormone levels and boost endorphins, the body's natural mood lifters. Exercise controls the production of stress hormones like cortisol and increases the levels of serotonin and dopamine, which can counter the symptoms of depression and anxiety.

• **Healthy Diet:** A healthy and balanced diet stabilizes blood sugar levels, which directly influences mood and energy. Proper nutrition means that your teen's body gets all the necessary nutrients to support hormonal balance. For instance, foods rich in Omega-3 fatty acids support brain health and can reduce anxiety and depression symptoms linked to hormonal changes. Besides eating healthy, it is also crucial to limit their intake of caffeinated products and sugary items. Any food that could disrupt their natural hormonal production is not good for their sensitivities.

• **Hydration:** Dehydration is responsible for affecting mood and cognitive function. It can exacerbate feelings of fatigue and irritability which makes it harder for your teen to cope with hormonal fluctuations. Keep reminding them throughout the day to drink more water.

• **Consistent Sleep Schedule:** A structured routine and fixed sleeping schedule are essential for every highly sensitive person, more so for teens. Sleep is responsible for regulating the production of their hormones and without a good 8 hours of sleep, their hormonal cycle gets messed up. Ask them to set up a consistent sleeping routine and follow it to maintain order and structure in their daily life.

High School Pressures

High school can be a tough time for many students because of the various pressures they face, including academic stress, peer pressure, and bullying. Highly sensitive teens feel these pressures even more strongly because of their sensitive nature.

A study called "The Power of Sensitivity: Empathy and Bullying among Adolescents" by Kim Samuel et al., from McGill University, explains why highly sensitive kids are affected more deeply. When highly sensitive teens encounter bullying or other unjust behaviors at school, they feel the pain more intensely than their peers. The study found that this intense emotional response is due to their heightened empathy, which amplifies the negative impact of bullying experiences.

The study also confirms that highly sensitive teens not only suffer from their own experiences of being bullied but also from witnessing the bullying of others. This dual burden leads to greater emotional distress and increases their risk of developing anxiety, depression, and other mental health issues. Their keen awareness of social dynamics and the emotional states of those around them means that school life can be particularly stressful for these kids.

In the light of such research studies, we can categorize their stress into the following:

Academic Stress

Getting good grades, doing well in sports and clubs, and preparing for college, there is ample stress when it comes to high school. This can make your teens feel anxious, sad, and worn out.

Highly sensitive kids feel academic stress even more because they think deeply about everything and can easily get overwhelmed by lots of work and high expectations. They worry more about what others think of them, which increases their stress.

Peer Pressure

Peer pressure is at its highest when kids enter their teens. They want to fit in and look cool in front of everyone at school. For HSCs, this pressure is even more intense as they cannot party like others just to fit in, knocking their confidence.

Bullying

Bullying is another serious problem in high school. It can make teens feel upset and alone which causes low self-esteem, anxiety, and depression.

How You Can Support Your Teen

So, what do these findings tell us? We need to recognize the unique challenges our highly sensitive adolescents face and create support systems tailored to their needs. While they need your help, they also need to experience their own autonomy and power of self-control.

It puts you in a difficult position but with smart strategies, you can help them through this rough transition.

Validate Their Feelings

The first thing your teens need to know is that their feelings are valid. Take time to listen to them when they express their concerns and experiences. Do not dismiss their worries and avoid telling them to "just relax." Instead, reassure them that it is okay to feel stressed and that you are there to support them. This gives them the confidence to deal with their teenage challenges.

Set Realistic Expectations

Help your teens set realistic goals for themselves academically. Break down larger tasks, such as studying for exams or completing big projects, into smaller, more manageable steps. Celebrate their achievements and progress along the way, no matter how small.

Offer Academic Support

Provide practical support to help your teens succeed academically. You can help them organize their study materials, create a study schedule, or find resources for extra help like online tutorials, courses, articles, and study forums. Give them the confidence to convey their concerns to their teachers if they are struggling with coursework.

Let Them Attain Balance

They need to maintain a healthy balance between schoolwork and other aspects of their lives. Ask them to participate in extracurricular activities as well. It does not have to be basketball or soccer; it can be any activity that makes them feel good about themselves like playing piano or learning ice skating. As a parent, you need to remind them that it is okay to prioritize their well-being and have fun, even during busy times.

Let Them Explore Their Autonomy

They need to feel that they can make decisions on their own and that you are not controlling their life. After providing them necessary help and guidance, give them the space to learn and unlearn different patterns and adjust their behaviors toward self-growth and development.

Be a Positive Role Model

Model healthy coping strategies and a positive attitude towards challenges. Show them that it is okay to ask for help when needed and that setbacks are a normal part of life. When you show resilience and perseverance in the face of adversity, it inspires and empowers your teens to do the same.

New Romantic Feelings and Relationships

Romantic feelings and relationships are developed in the teenage years. Highly sensitive teens experience those emotions more intensely and anything that happens in a relationship may also affect them at a far deeper level, making them more susceptible to hurt and feelings of distress. This sensitivity is both a blessing and a curse, depending on how they learn to deal with and regulate their emotions. Rose Sherman's study, "To Love a Highly Sensitive a Highly Sensitive Person: A Theoretical Study on Romantic Relationships and Sensitivity" also examines how HSP traits fit into romantic relationships.

Intense Emotional Awareness

Highly sensitive kids process experiences and emotions on a much deeper level than non-HSPs, which means that their romantic feelings are often more intense and profound. This heightened sensitivity allows them to experience the joys and sorrows of love in a more magnified way. When in love, highly sensitive people feel an overwhelming sense of connection and passion, as their brains are wired to notice and be affected by the subtleties in their partner's behavior and emotional states.

Empathy and Connection

Empathy is a key trait of these kids, which means they can deeply understand and resonate with their partner's emotions. This ability to empathize enhances the emotional bond in a relationship, as HSPs are often very attuned to their partner's needs and feelings. However, this same empathy can also lead to emotional overload, as they might absorb and internalize their partner's stress or negative emotions, intensifying their own emotional experiences.

Communication and Intimacy

Sherman's study suggests that in a successful romantic relationship, highly sensitive people rely heavily on communication and intimacy. They thrive in relationships where open and honest communication is prioritized. Their ability to tell what they need and understand their partner's feelings can lead to a rich, shared intimacy. This deep level of communication helps in addressing and managing the intense emotions that come with their heightened sensitivity.

Overarousal and Overstimulation

One of the challenges for highly sensitive people in romantic relationships is their susceptibility to overarousal and overstimulation. They become easily overwhelmed by too much sensory input or emotional stress, which can affect their relationship dynamics. They have to recognize and manage these thresholds for the well-being of their relationship. They should communicate their limits and take time to recharge so that their sensitivity does not lead to chronic stress or burnout.

Mutual Understanding and Compassion

The success of an HSP's relationship depends significantly on mutual understanding and compassion. Partners of HSPs have to be super empathetic and understanding of their sensitivity, to create an environment where they can feel safe and supported. This mutual understanding helps in regulating the intense emotions and potential conflicts that may arise due to the HSP's heightened sensitivity.

Positive Interactions

According to Sherman's research, a high ratio of positive to negative interactions (5:1) is a must for HSPs to thrive in a successful relationship. They need more positive interactions like expressions of love, appreciation, and support for emotional stability and satisfaction. These positive experiences can counterbalance the intensity of their emotions and foster a nurturing and resilient relationship.

Guiding Them Through First Relationships

First relationships are always challenging for teens because they experience everything intensely for the first time. The highs and lows, the excitement and heartbreak, all feel incredibly profound and new. As adults, we must recognize and respect the depth of their feelings rather than dismissing them as merely emotional or childish. It is our job to help them identify their emotions and advise them on how to deal with them without getting overwhelmed or confused. Here is what you can do:

Help Them Understand Their Sensitivity

Explain that their sensitivities can affect their future relationships and let them understand that their deep emotional experiences and empathy are strengths that can enrich their relationships. They should see their sensitivity as a natural gift and not a flaw. This way they will learn to respect their own feelings and the need for space and boundaries.

Communicate Their Needs

Not being able to express their needs clearly in a relationship often leaves HSPs in an unfulfilling and emotionally draining relationship. It is their innate empathy that makes them put their partner's needs above their own, however, this may take a great toll on their emotional well being. Teach them how to openly express their needs and define boundaries by engaging them in role-play conversations where they can learn to practice articulating their emotions and setting boundaries. Remind them that being honest about their sensitivity with their partner is not selfish but rather an act of love and mutual understanding.

Manage Overarousal and Overstimulation

There are often situations in a relationship that may lead to emotional overload for an HSP. Some examples include:

- Loud voices, intense emotions, and confrontational behavior during conflicts

- Large gatherings with lots of people, noise, and activity

- Family gatherings involving many relatives or high levels of emotional drama

- Excessive or public displays of affection

- Crowded restaurants, noisy public places, or bustling events

- Relationships that demand constant social interaction without adequate downtime

- Relationships involving high emotional drama, intense exchanges, or frequent emotional highs and lows

- Partners or friends who invade personal space, disregard boundaries, or demand immediate responses

- Unpredictable schedules, sudden changes, or a lack of routine

Teach them ways to avoid and manage such situations by employing coping mechanisms like taking a break, deep breathing, and communicating their needs to their partner.

Positive Interactions

Teach your teen the importance of maintaining a high ratio of positive to negative interactions in their relationships. Ask them to focus on positive expressions of love, appreciation, and support and convey their needs to their partner. Positive interactions can help balance their intense emotions and create a nurturing relationship environment.

Healthy Boundaries

Your teen must understand the importance of setting healthy boundaries in their relationships. Tell them that it's okay to say no and set limits. They should know that no relationship is worth sacrificing their mental health, emotional well-being, self-respect, need for space, sleep, life goals, and routine. Emphasize that respecting their own boundaries and those of their partner is key to a healthy relationship.

Dealing with Heartbreak

Though extremely hurtful, they are not always avoidable, and your highly sensitive teen needs to understand this reality. They have to keep their mind and emotions ready and prepared for such an overstimulating situation. They will intensely feel the hurt and their empathy for their partner might make it difficult for them to move on. You can help by telling them that it's normal to feel sad, disappointed, and heartbroken, and reassuring them that their emotions are legitimate. You can encourage them to practice self-care by spending time with supportive friends and family, engaging in hobbies, exercising, and practicing mindfulness. Remind them that healing always takes time and that it is fine to grieve the end of the relationship. With patience and reassurance, they will eventually feel better. Help them see that breakups are a chance to learn and grow. Make a point to have weekly check-ins to discuss their feelings and relationship experiences. These regular conversations can provide them with the support and understanding they need.

Let's take Annie, for example, a highly sensitive teen who experienced her first romantic relationship in high school. She poured her heart and soul into the relationship, feeling deeply connected to her partner. However, when the relationship ended unexpectedly, she was devastated. She felt overwhelmed by intense emotions of sadness and rejection. With the support of her parents, Annie gradually learned to cope with heartbreak. She leaned on her friends and family for emotional support, finding comfort in their presence and understanding. Annie also immersed herself in activities she loved, such as painting and playing music, which provided solace during difficult times. As time passed, Annie slowly began to heal from the heartbreak. She gained valuable insights into herself and her needs in a relationship. While the breakup was challenging, she emerged stronger and more resilient, ready to embrace the next chapter of her romantic journey with courage and optimism.

Bottom Line

In this chapter, we explored the unique challenges that highly sensitive teens face as they step into this new phase of their lives. We examined the intense emotions and deep experiences they encounter, especially when developing their first relationships. Here, I have discussed key strategies like effective communication, managing overstimulation, setting healthy boundaries, fostering positive interactions, building emotional resilience, and practicing regular self-care.

Your support through this phase is vital. Their heightened sensitivity means they will experience emotions more intensely, and dismissing their feelings can be harmful. So, empathize with them, understand their experiences, validate their emotions, and give them the coping tools that can help them develop emotional resilience and self-awareness.

Exercises/Activities

Share the following activities with your highly sensitive teen and engage them to counter their feelings of overwhelm, stress, and anxiety:

Breathing Sessions

Set aside time each day and sit with your child in a soothing environment for a short session of deep breathing exercises. Try the 4-7-8 technique in which you inhale for 4 seconds, hold your breath for 7 seconds, and exhale for 8 seconds. Repeat it for at least 2-3 minutes to induce calm.

Journaling Prompts

Ask your teen to write about their day using prompts such as "What made me feel happy today?" or "What challenged me today and how did I handle it?" It will give them an outlet for processing emotions and gaining insights into their experiences.

Art Therapy

Arrange a small art workshop at home and engage your teens in creative activities of their choice whether it's pottery, painting, playing music or crafting. It is a great way to spend quality time together while helping them process their emotions through non-verbal expression.

Chapter 9

FOSTERING RESILIENCE IN YOUR HIGH SENSITIVE CHILD

"Resilience is knowing that you are the only one that has the power and the responsibility to pick yourself up." — Mary Holloway

You become resilient when you learn to recover from setbacks and adapt well to change. It is a superpower that keeps you going in the face of adversity.

Resilience is particularly crucial for highly sensitive kids, who deeply feel emotions and are more attuned to subtle environmental changes. It helps them manage their intense emotions, cope with social pressures, and adapt to new situations without becoming overwhelmed. With resilience, they can also counter their overstimulation, build confidence, and develop a strong sense of self-worth. Once you teach your kid to grow into a resilient being, they will be able to turn their sensitivity into strength and take on all life's challenges like a rock.

Take Lucas for instance, who is a highly sensitive teenager at the school where a friend of mine teaches history. Lucas struggled when his parents went through a tough divorce, and his grades began to slip because he felt overwhelmed by his emotions. His school counselor saw his sensitivity as a strength and helped him find ways to cope. She introduced him to journaling and mindfulness techniques, which helped him manage his stress. She also encouraged Lucas to join the art club, where he found a passion for painting. With her support and these effective tools, Lucas regained his confidence, improved his grades, and began to thrive.

His story shows how resilience and the right support can help highly sensitive kids overcome challenges and succeed. By using similar interventions and tools your kid can also learn to be resilient.

Understanding Resilience in Highly Sensitive Children

Highly sensitive kids are naturally super resilient, they just need some help to discover their inner strength. In Elaine N. Aron's book "The Highly Sensitive Child: Helping Our Children Thrive When the World Overwhelms Them," she discusses the concept of high sensitivity and its impact on resilience in children. According to Aron, Highly Sensitive Children show resilience in unique ways compared to non-HSC children. We just need to discover how!

Heightened Awareness

These kids are more attuned to subtle changes in their environment, whether it's social dynamics, emotions, or sensory stimuli, they all affect them deeply. This heightened awareness allows them to adapt more quickly to changes and challenges, which is a sign of resilience.

Deeper Processing

Since HSCs tend to process information more deeply and reflect on their experiences with greater intensity, they gain valuable insights from difficult situations and understand how to deal with them. Ultimately, this practice fosters resilience.

Emotional Agility

HSCs have greater emotional agility, so they become apt at recognizing, understanding, and regulating their emotions. This emotional intelligence equips them with the tools to cope with stress, setbacks, and disappointments and gives them wings to bounce back from adversity with resilience.

Aron's research suggests that resilience in highly sensitive kids is not solely about bouncing back from adversity but also about embracing their sensitivity as a valuable asset. You can provide them with support and guidance to help develop self-awareness, emotional intelligence, and social connections to harness their unique qualities and overcome challenges in their personal and academic lives.

The Role of Parents in Building Resilience

Highly sensitive kids require a supportive and nurturing environment to become stronger and more resilient to deal with everyday challenges. Research supports the idea that parental behavior and attitudes significantly influence a child's ability to develop resilience. One relevant study is by Dr. Ann S. Masten, a renowned psychologist who has extensively studied resilience in children. According to Dr. Ann S. Masten's research, resilience is not an extraordinary trait but rather an ordinary one that can be nurtured through supportive relationships. Masten's studies highlight several key factors through which parents can play their part and instill resilience in their children:

Modeling Resilient Behavior

Parents who show resilient behaviors in the face of adversity provide a powerful example for their kids. This includes handling stress calmly, seeking solutions to problems, and maintaining a positive outlook despite challenges.

Emotional Support

Emotional support from parents, in the form of active listening, validating feelings, and offering encouragement, helps children feel secure and valued, which is essential for building resilience.

Problem-Solving Skills

Parents who encourage their children to tackle challenges and solve problems independently help them build confidence and problem-solving skills. This approach is perfect to create a sense of competence and autonomy in them.

Positive Relationships

Developing a strong, supportive parent-child relationship is also important here. Masten's research suggests that kids who have a close and trusting relationship with their parents are more likely to develop resilience.

A Stable Environment

Stability at home, including consistent routines and clear expectations, provides a secure base for Highly Sensitive Children. This stability allows them to explore, take risks, and learn from their experiences without fear of excessive consequences.

One of Masten's notable studies is "Project Competence,"

which examined resilience in children over several decades. The study found that children who had supportive and nurturing parents were more likely to develop resilience and succeed despite facing significant adversities. All of those findings point us in the right direction! That is to provide support, care, and necessary coping tools to our kids to make them resilient.

Strategies for Fostering Resilience

It was not just Masten's findings that highlighted the role of parents in developing resilience in kids. Nancy Eisenberg et al also did some great work on similar topics, studying the strategies that can be most useful to instill resilience in kids. According to "Parenting and the Development of Effortful Control from Early Childhood to Early Adolescence: A Transactional Developmental Model", there are several ways parents can effectively support their Highly Sensitive Children in building resilience. Such as:

1. Emotional Regulation

You can teach them how to recognize and manage their emotions in healthy ways (refer to chapter 02 of this book). Eisenberg et al.'s study emphasizes that parents who respond sensitively to their children's emotions and provide consistent guidance help foster the development of effortful control, which is essential for resilience.

2. Problem-Solving Skills

You can even support your kids in finding solutions to various problems, breaking tasks into manageable steps, and persevering in the face of setbacks. If you exhibit better problem-solving skills in front of them, it will develop a growth mindset and empower your children to tackle challenges with confidence and resilience.

3. Coping Strategies

Helping Highly Sensitive Children develop effective coping strategies is essential for building resilience. You can teach them a variety of coping techniques, like mindfulness, positive self-talk, and getting social support. By providing them with a toolbox of coping strategies, you can empower your kids to deal with daily stressors and setbacks with resilience and adaptability.

4. Supportive Environment

Eisenberg et al.'s study also highlights the importance of warm, responsive parenting practices in promoting the development of effortful control and emotional regulation. You can provide them love, encouragement, and consistent support to feel safe and secure, which lays the foundation for resilience.

5. Encouraging Independence

To help your Highly Sensitive Child develop confidence and resilience, encourage their autonomy and independence in ways that are suitable for their age. You can do this by gradually increasing your child's responsibilities and providing opportunities for them to make decisions and solve problems independently without your constant involvement.

6. Promote Emotional Expression

It is essential to let your child express their feelings freely without fear of judgment or criticism. When children feel safe to share their emotions, they develop better coping mechanisms for stress and adversity. If children are allowed to talk openly about their feelings, they become more adept at handling stress. Providing a supportive and non-judgmental space can help HSCs build emotional resilience.

Bottom Line

In this chapter, we particularly explored the idea the developing resilience in highly sensitive kids to help them with life's challenges. Simply by recognizing their heightened emotional responses and empathic inclinations, you can establish a super nurturing atmosphere required for emotional expression, developing coping mechanisms, problem-solving prowess, and a sense of security. You just have to embrace your child's sensitivity and offer them steadfast guidance.

Remember, it requires your utmost patience and perseverance to instill the power of resilience into your kids. It is an ongoing journey that will require your constant attention toward your child's apprehensions, unwavering encouragement, and support.

Don't forget to celebrate your own achievements and the wins of your child. Cherishing little moments together will create a strong and trustable bond between you and your kids. This bond is the actual foundation of resilience. Through this nurturing relationship, you can ensure your child's emotional well-being and cultivate a conducive environment for your HSC to flourish in all their endeavors.

Exercises/Activities

Want your kid to strongly face life's challenges? Here are some powerful yet simple activities that they can enjoy and use to explore their inner strengths:

Problem-Solving Board Game

Play a problem-solving board game like "The Game of Life" or "Finding the Clues." Create fake scenarios or use riddles and ask your child to find a solution to the problems. Throughout the game, you can encourage your child to strategize and adapt to unexpected challenges to reinforce resilience in navigating obstacles.

Gratitude Jar

Decorate a jar with your child and place it in a visible location. Each day, take turns writing down something you are grateful for on a small piece of paper and put it in the jar. At the end of the week, read the notes together and discuss how focusing on gratitude can help build resilience.

Role-Playing Social Scenarios

Act out different social situations with your child, such as inviting a new friend to play, politely saying NO to a friend for a game night, or resolving a conflict with a sibling. Practice assertive communication and problem-solving skills with them to develop confidence and resilience in social interactions.

Chapter 10

SUPPORTING YOUR HIGHLY SENSITIVE CHILD THROUGH LIFE CHANGES

"The secret of change is to focus all of your energy not on fighting the old, but on building the new." - Socrates

Naturally, we all have varying tendencies to accept change. Some people are apt at going with the flow, while others face difficulty dealing with new situations.

Since Highly Sensitive Children are uniquely attuned to their surroundings and find comfort in routine, they often react more intensely to changes than other kids. They pick up on subtle cues, experience emotions deeply, and can feel overwhelmed by unexpected situations. Given their heightened sensitivity, it is essential to provide them with solid support and guidance to deal with any transition in life.

Change is inevitable and we should raise our children to be comfortable with this. Instead of avoiding change, they can be taught how to embrace it without jeopardizing their life goals and emotional or physical well-being. This is why, in this chapter, we will explore how change affects HSCs and how we can better prepare for various unforeseen circumstances.

Understanding Change from an HSC's Perspective

We have established the fact that highly sensitive kids perceive and process changes differently due to their heightened sensitivity which affects their cognitive and emotional responses to stimuli. They tend to feel joy, excitement, sadness, and anxiety more profoundly than their less sensitive peers. And from the work of Elaine Aron's book, we can infer that HSCs take in and analyze information from their environment more deeply than others and they consider multiple facets of a situation before making decisions. This deep sensory processing allows them to make thoughtful and informed choices, often seeing connections and details that others might miss. However, this can also leave them feeling overwhelmed by excessive information or rapid changes. The constant influx of details requires great mental energy, which can lead to fatigue and stress when they cannot process everything at their own pace. The need to process these subtle stimuli continuously can lead to sensory overload and increased stress levels. That is why you see an HSC reacting more strongly to change. Whether it is changing their home, switching schools or even changing their routine, they need time to process and accept every new situation.

Relocation and HSCs

Moving to a new place can stir up a lot of emotions in highly sensitive kids. They feel anxious and fearful about the uncertainties that come with relocating. Worries about leaving behind familiar surroundings, friends, and routines, as well as the unknown aspects of their new environment, can cause huge stress. Alongside anxiety, they may also experience strong feelings of sadness and grief, while mourning the loss of their old home, school, and community. The sense of loss and nostalgia can be powerful. The entire process, from packing and saying goodbye to traveling and settling into a new home, can lead to extreme sensory overload and overstimulation. You then see this stress and anxiety in the form of increased irritability, withdrawal, moodiness, or regressive behaviors like bedwetting or thumb-sucking, especially in younger children.

Despite these challenges, some highly sensitive kids also feel a mix of excitement and curiosity about the move. They could look forward to exploring new surroundings, making new friends, and experiencing different opportunities. However, the upheaval of moving can disrupt their sleep patterns, leading to difficulty falling asleep, staying asleep, or experiencing nightmares. Physical symptoms related to stress and anxiety like headaches, stomachaches, or muscle tension, further exacerbate this discomfort. Social withdrawal or reluctance to engage in new social interactions is another potential reaction, as they feel overwhelmed by the prospect of making new friends or hesitant to participate in unfamiliar social situations.

Either way, relocation can trigger a sense of disorientation as they go through this transition from the familiar to the unfamiliar. It is challenging for them to adjust to new routines, landmarks, and cultural norms. They need your time, patience, and understanding to feel secure and comfortable in their new environment.

Strategies to Cope with Relocation

There are plenty of steps you can take before the relocation to make your kids feel safe and comfortable. The aim is to make this change less overwhelming for them. My advice is to slowly prepare them for the move and not drop the news out of the blue. Be gentle and kind!

Familiarize Them with the New Environment

If possible, visit the new area before the move to familiarize them with their new surroundings. Take a walk around the neighborhood, visit the local park, and drive by the new school to help them get a feel for the area. Introduce your kid to new neighbors, classmates, or community members if possible. Organize playdates or meetups with local families to help your children make connections and feel more comfortable in their new environment.

Show your children where important amenities are located, such as grocery stores, libraries, and medical facilities. Knowing where to find essential services can help dismiss some of their concerns about the move.

You can also use online resources like Google Maps, virtual tours, or websites of local attractions to explore the new neighborhood, school, and community together. Show your children important landmarks, parks, playgrounds, and places of interest. Take photos or videos of the new home, school, and surroundings to show your children what to expect. Point out features they might find interesting or exciting, such as a nearby playground or a favorite restaurant.

Discuss Transportation

Talk to your children about transportation options in the new area like bus routes, walking paths, or bike trails. If applicable, practice walking or biking to nearby destinations together to help them feel more confident about getting around.

Focus on the positive aspects of the new location and highlight opportunities for new experiences and adventures. Be open and honest about any concerns or questions they may have about the move. Listen actively to their feelings and validate their emotions to provide reassurance and support along the way.

Acknowledge Their Feelings about Relocation

Let them know that it is okay to feel anxious, sad, or scared about leaving behind their familiar surroundings and starting anew. Give them constant reassurance that their feelings are normal and understandable given the circumstances. Ask them to express their emotions openly and assure them that you are there to support and comfort them throughout the transition.

Involve Them in the Process

Give your kids a sense of empowerment by involving them in the moving process. Let them participate in packing their belongings, sorting through their possessions, and making decisions about what to bring to the new home. Provide them opportunities to share their ideas and preferences, such as choosing paint colors for their new room or selecting furniture arrangements. This participation will also take their mind away from the overwhelm.

Maintain Routines and Familiarity

During the move, strive to maintain consistency in familiar routines and rituals. Stick to regular meal times, bedtime routines, and other daily rituals that your children are most familiar with. These fixed routines will give them a sense of stability and comfort during times of transition. They will help anchor your children during the uncertainty of the move. Consistency in familiar activities can also help reduce their stress and anxiety.

Create a Comforting Space

Select a special space in your new home that feels comforting for them. This can be their own bedroom. Ask them to decorate it with familiar belongings like their favorite stuffed animals, posters, or favorite toys. You can participate in this activity as well. Create a cozy corner or reading nook where they can retreat to relax and unwind. Fill this space with items that cultivate positive memories and feelings.

Changing Schools

Another big change that can affect HSCs is the change of schools. It often happens along with the relocation, so together these changes can really be taxing for a highly sensitive kid.

The idea of leaving behind their friends, familiar teachers, and a known environment can be distressing and trigger feelings of sadness, loss, and separation anxiety. Highly sensitive kids are keenly aware of social dynamics and often develop close friendships. Adjusting to any new social environment can be overwhelming as they face unfamiliar social cues, peer relationships, and group dynamics. The anxiety about the unknown aspects of a new school like unfamiliar teachers, classmates, routines, and academic expectations, can exacerbate their feelings of fear and insecurity.

For HSCs, a new school means exposure to different sensory stimuli, new classroom layouts, noise levels, and routines, and that can be too much for their senses. Moreover, there is also academic pressure to perform in a new setting, where they perceive high expectations from teachers, parents, or peers which intensify their stress and anxiety and negatively affect their confidence and self-esteem. These kids thrive on familiarity and routine, and the disruption caused by changing schools can unsettle their sense of stability and security.

How to prepare your child for this transition

Again, like any big transition, the change of school is more frightening for HSCs, and they need your help in this regard. If you make their next school a little familiar, they will find it easier to adjust to the new setting. For that, you can try certain interventions:

Visit the School Together

Before classes start, take your kid to their new school. Explore the school building, classrooms, cafeteria, library, and playground with. Let them meet their new teacher and see where they will be spending their time as it helps reduce their anxiety about the unknown and make the new environment feel more familiar.

Discuss Their Fears

Talk to them about their fears and concerns regarding the transition. Ask them to express their feelings and listen intently. If they have any specific worries, provide them with relevant information to clear out any confusion or ambiguity.

Create a Transition Plan

Work together to create a plan for the first few weeks at the new school. Discuss with your kids whether they want your help to pack their school bags, or simply ask what they might want to do during breaks and then create a comfortable morning routine around their level of comfort. A good and well-thought plan provides every highly sensitive kid with a sense of control and structure, which is comforting for during any major transition.

Encourage Healthy Connections

Without forcing your child to socialize, ask them to gradually build new social connections. You can arrange social playdates with their potential new classmates or neighbors. They can join clubs or after-school activities to get to know the kids they will be seeing in their new classroom.

Highlight Positive Aspects

Highlight the positive aspects of the new school and mention all the new opportunities. Talk about activities, clubs, or subjects that might interest your child. Present this transition as a great way to look forward to new experiences and adventures, this will shift their perspective from what they are leaving behind to what they can gain.

Practice New Routines

If possible, practice the new school routine before their first day. Walk or drive the route to school, discuss where they will be dropped off and picked up, and go over what their day might look like. Familiarity with these morning routines can significantly reduce their anxiety on the first day.

Divorce and Separation

Going through a parental divorce can be tough, especially for highly sensitive kids. They are emotional sponges who soak up all the vibes around them, and whenever there is tension or conflict between their parents, they can feel it like a storm brewing inside them. They already deal with anxiety, guilt, and sadness while trying to deal with their sensitivities, so when they get any hint of discord in the house, it can really mess with their heads. They might feel torn between mom and dad, not sure where to turn or who to side with. It can feel like being stuck in an emotional tug-of-war!

Plus, highly sensitive kids thrive on routine and stability, so when the family dynamic changes, they can see their safe haven getting shattered in front of their own eyes. Suddenly, everything feels uncertain, and that can really ramp up their anxiety levels. And let's not forget about the tricky business of parental alienation. With their big hearts and tendency to take things to heart, they can be easily influenced by one parent to see the other in a negative light. It's a tough spot to be in, and it can mess with their ability to trust and form healthy relationships down the line.

"Divorce Poison," by Richard Warshak also explores the similar phenomenon of parental alienation and its impact on children during and after divorce. The disruption of their familiar environment and routines can amplify their anxiety and emotional distress.

So, what is the solution? They need loads of reassurance and support from both parents. Divorce can be traumatizing for couples, and it can feel challenging to keep yourself calm and composed during this testing time.

But, when you are raising a highly sensitive kid, you will have to think about their emotional well-being at every step of the way, otherwise, it might leave a lasting impact on their minds. They will need all your help to weather the storm and come out stronger on the other side.

Strategies for Maintaining Stability

The upheaval and changes associated with divorce can deeply affect their emotional well-being, as they may internalize the conflicts and tensions between their parents. This heightened sensitivity can exacerbate their emotional responses, leading to feelings of anxiety, sadness, and insecurity. Therefore, it is crucial to approach discussions about divorce with great care and sensitivity.

Break the News at the Right Time and Place

Select a quiet, private setting where you and your child can have an undisturbed conversation. Timing matters: choose a moment when your child is relaxed and receptive, avoiding discussions during times of stress or upheaval.

Be Honest and Age-Appropriate

Communicate in clear, simple language suitable for your child's age and understanding. Be honest about the reasons for the divorce or separation without assigning blame or delving into unnecessary details.

Ask Them About Their Feelings

After explaining the situation to them, make sure to take their opinions on the subject and how they feel about it. Let them know it's normal to feel sad, angry, confused, or scared. Give them opportunities to express their anger and frustration.

Reassure Them of Your Love

No matter what happens, your child must be assured that they are loved and cherished and that the divorce or separation is not their fault. Reaffirm that both parents will continue to love and support them during and after the divorce.

Questions and Open Communication

Create an atmosphere where your child feels comfortable asking questions and sharing their thoughts and feelings. Listen attentively, validate their concerns about divorce, and provide honest, age-appropriate answers to their queries. Tell them clearly what will happen after the divorce and how you and your partner will ensure that their daily life will not be affected by this decision.

Strategies for Maintaining Stability During This Time

Stick to familiar routines and schedules as much as possible to provide a sense of stability and predictability for your child. The more regularity you will maintain for their meal times, bedtime rituals, and other daily routines the more grounded they will feel amidst the changes.

Co-parenting After Separation or Divorce

Healthy and mindful co-parenting after separation or divorce is not just a choice but a necessity, especially when your child is highly sensitive. At this point, your child might feel torn between parents and find themselves stuck in limbo. Not being able to live with both parents is traumatic, and any additional conflict may take a huge toll on their mental health.

This is the time to minimize conflict and tension and to lay out a co-parenting strategy with your ex-partner. Take every decision according to the sensitivities of your kids and provide a fixed consistent routine with no drastic changes.

Stay in Touch

Keep lines of communication open with your ex-partner regarding your child's needs and feelings. Collaborate on important decisions related to your child's upbringing, such as schooling, healthcare, and extracurricular activities. Regular communication keeps both parents involved and informed.

Establish Consistent Routines

Consistency is key for HSCs, as it provides them with a sense of stability and predictability. Initially, try to manage and keep them in the same setting without any displacement. First, let them process the family dynamic after the divorce then slowly introduce other changes into their lives. Coordinate with your ex-partner to maintain consistent routines across both households. They should be able to follow the same routine at both houses.

Practice Patience and Flexibility

Understand that adjusting to new family dynamics may take time for your HSC. Be patient and flexible, give them the space and time they need to adapt. Offer your support and reassurance throughout the transition period, and be prepared to adjust your co-parenting approach as needed.

Maintain Respectful Communication

Despite any disagreements that may arise, maintain respectful communication with your ex-partner, especially in front of your child. Remember that children learn from observing adult behavior, so modeling respectful communication sets a positive example for your child.

Create Safe Spaces in Both Homes

Both homes should provide safe spaces where your HSC can retreat when feeling overwhelmed. Set up a quiet corner or their own room filled with comforting items like books and art supplies. Let them use this safe space to decompress and manage their emotions effectively.

Regularly Review and Adjust Co-Parenting Plans

As your child grows and their needs change, regularly review and adjust your co-parenting plans with your ex-partner. Flexibility and adaptability are important here. Your child's evolving needs must be met. Regular communication with your ex-partner is essential to facilitate this process.

Single Parenting

Single parenting poses unique challenges while raising Highly Sensitive Children as it can be emotionally and physically taxing.

One significant challenge is managing the emotional intensity of your Highly Sensitive Child without the support of a partner. You may find it overwhelming to address your child's intense emotional reactions while also dealing with their feelings, which can be exhausting

Without the support of a co-parent, you may feel the weight of increased responsibility, which leads to stress, burnout, and isolation. Limited access to a support system further compounds these challenges, as single parents may have fewer resources for assistance and respite. Financial strain is another significant hurdle, as single parents may struggle to make ends meet on a single income, adding financial stress to their already demanding responsibilities. Balancing work commitments with parenting duties can also be challenging.

So, if you are a single parent who is raising an HSC, the first thing you need to do is take all the help you can get. Your emotional well-being is important for the mental wellness of your kid. The stronger and more confident you feel, the happier and healthier your child will be. There is nothing wrong in leaning on family members, friends, or community organizations for both emotional and practical assistance. Join support groups or online communities for single parents to get valuable advice, encouragement, and a sense of solidarity with others facing similar challenges.

Practice mindful techniques, exercises, and calming activities to release stress. Make time for activities that help you recharge and alleviate stress, whether it's through exercise, meditation, pursuing hobbies, or spending time with supportive friends or family members. Taking care of yourself allows you to better support your child's needs.

Moreover, you can take advantage of community resources and services available in your area. Many communities offer childcare assistance programs, parenting classes, or support groups specifically tailored to the needs of single parents and families with Highly Sensitive Children. These resources can provide valuable guidance and support as you navigate the challenges of single parenthood.

Coping with Loss

Whether it is the loss of a toy, pet, or favorite person, it leaves a profound impact on HSCs. Like all other emotions, HSCs also feel loss more intensely than others.

According to the research study "Helping Children Cope with Loss, Death, and Grief" by Ryan P. Kilmer, the empathetic nature of highly sensitive kids makes them a walking grief magnet. They not only feel sadness for themselves, but they can experience the pain of others as well, which increases their intensity of grief. This amplifies their emotional distress and complicates their ability to cope with the loss.

HSCs also struggle to accept the permanence of loss, particularly in the case of death. Their sensitive nature makes it challenging for them to comprehend the finality of death, leading to prolonged feelings of confusion and longing. The disruption of familiar routines and stability further increases their anxiety and complicates their grief process.

To help HSCs process grief and heal, it is crucial to provide strategies that cater to their heightened sensitivity. Firstly, let them express their feelings in a safe and supportive environment. Give them reassurance and validation to make them feel that they are understood and supported during this challenging time.

Keep their routines consistent to offer a sense of security amidst the upheaval of loss, while also providing a familiar anchor for HSCs to rely on. Plus, you can involve them in rituals or activities that honor the memory of what or who was lost to provide comfort and closure.

Ultimately, you will have to create an environment where your highly sensitive kids feel heard, supported, and validated so they can process grief and step into a healing journey.

Some kids do not like to talk about their grief after losing someone, simply because it is too overwhelming for them to put their feelings into words. It's okay if they don't talk about it, don't force them to do so. You can instead give them a writing journal to record their thoughts, feelings, and memories related to the loss. Writing is a great therapeutic outlet for expressing emotions and processing their grief in a private and introspective way.

Another good way to help HSCs process their emotion is to help them create a memory box or scrapbook where they can collect photos, mementos, and keepsakes. This tangible representation of memories can offer them comfort and a positive way to honor their relationship with the lost loved one. Alternatively, you can also engage them in activities that would honor the memory of the person or thing that was lost, such as planting a tree, lighting a candle, or creating a special piece of artwork.

These rituals give them a sense of closure and allow HSCs to express their love and appreciation for what they have lost.

Bottom Line

As you journey through these changes with your child, remember that your calm presence and understanding words are their guiding light. Be patient with them—and yourself—because navigating change is a process, not a sprint. Your compassion is their comfort, helping them feel safe and supported no matter what comes their way.

So, embrace this role with confidence. Celebrate the small

victories, be there for the tough days, and know that your efforts are planting the seeds for a resilient and thriving future.

You've got this, and more importantly, so does your child. Let's keep moving forward together, one compassionate step at a time!

Chapter 11

CONCLUSION

"Encourage your empathic child to see their sensitivity as a strength, for it is their greatest gift." — Elaine N. Aron

As we wrap up this journey into the world of parenting Highly Sensitive Children, let's take a moment to reflect on the key insights and strategies we have explored together. This book began by introducing the concept of sensitivity, helping you understand the unique ways in which HSCs perceive and react to the world around them. We looked into the challenges that come with parenting these special children and acknowledged the extra layers of care and attention they require.

We explored the causes of high sensitivity, from genetic predispositions to environmental influences, giving you a comprehensive understanding of why your child might experience the world more intensely. Recognizing these causes is the first step toward empathy and effective support.

Throughout the chapters, I offered a detailed roadmap to raise your Highly Sensitive Child with confidence and compassion. There are strategies to help your child develop emotional literacy, enabling them to understand and express their feelings in healthy ways. The emphasis remained on the importance of building resilience and teaching your child to navigate life's ups and downs with strength and grace.

Setting boundaries was another crucial aspect we covered to let you know how to create a structured yet nurturing environment that respects your child's sensitivity while encouraging their independence. Here, I highlighted the significant role of diet, exercise, and sleep in managing sensitivities and offered practical tips to ensure your child's physical well-being supports their emotional health.

Coping with stress, change, and loss is an inevitable part of life, especially for HSCs. There are actionable steps for your child to manage these challenges, from stress-reducing techniques to preparing for and adapting to change. Building strong, supportive relationships was also a key focus, as these connections are vital for your child's emotional security and growth.

This book offers a detailed roadmap for raising Highly Sensitive Children, offering practical, compassionate, and effective strategies to support their growth. By following the guidance provided, you can help your child not only manage their sensitivity but also harness it as a source of strength and creativity.

Your warm support is crucial in helping your HSC become a strong and resilient individual. By employing the strategies shared in this book, you will be equipping your child with the tools they need to thrive. Your patience, understanding, and dedication will develop a sense of security and confidence in your child.

Every review matters, and I would really appreciate your support in leaving an honest review.

Your views on this book and your insights can provide invaluable support to other parents facing similar challenges. Reviews are critical for getting books in front of readers. It elevates visibility, and your review would serve as a beacon, guiding others to discover the inspiration and guidance they are looking for. Before leaving, I would like to ask you to share your feedback on this book and your experiences in parenting your Highly Sensitive Child by leaving a review on Amazon.

Leaving a Review is Effortless: Scan the QR Code below or visit your Amazon order page, click on *Write a Review*, and share your thoughts about this book.

Amazon US:

Amazon UK:

Amazon Australia:

Amazon Canada:

Don't forget to download

YOUR BONUS GIFT

Companion Workbook & Journal

Simply scan the QR code below

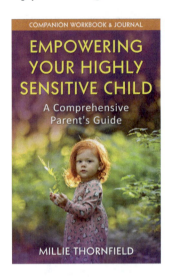

RESOURCES

Some great reads to learn more about parenting Highly Sensitive Children:

- *The Essential Beginner's Guide to Meditation & Mindfulness* by Rohini Heendeniya

- *Quiet Kids: Helping Your Introverted Child Thrive in an Extroverted World* by Christine Fonseca

- *Sensitive and Strong: A Guide for Highly Sensitive Persons and Those Who Love Them* by Barrie S. Jaeger

- *The Empath's Survival Guide: Life Strategies for Sensitive People* by Judith Orloff

- *The Highly Sensitive Child: Helping Our Children Thrive When the World Overwhelms Them* by Elaine N. Aron

- *The Highly Sensitive Person: How to Thrive When the World Overwhelms You* by Elaine N. Aron

- *Calm Parents, Happy Kids: The Secrets of Stress-free Parenting* by Laura Markham

- *Emotional Intelligence: Why It Can Matter More Than IQ* by Daniel Goleman

- *Highly Sensitive Kids: Helping Your Child Thrive When the World Overwhelms Them* by Stacey Nyman

- *Parenting the Highly Sensitive Child: Guide to Positive Parenting, Understanding Your Child's Emotions, and Helping Them Thrive* by Julie B. Rosenshein

- *Quiet: The Power of Introverts in a World That Can't Stop Talking* by Susan Cain

- *Raising an Anxious Child: How to Help Your Child Conquer Fear and Anxiety* by Dr. David Lewis

- *Sensitive Is the New Strong: The Power of Empaths in an Increasingly Harsh World* by Anita Moorjani

- *The Empathic Parent's Guide to Raising a Highly Sensitive Child* by Freeda Meighan

- *The Mindful Child: How to Help Your Kid Manage Stress and Become Happier, Kinder, and More Compassionate* by Susan Kaiser Greenland

- *The Strong, Sensitive Boy: Help Your Son Build Healthy Emotions Without Coddling or Criticizing* by Ted Zeff

- *The Whole-Brain Child: 12 Revolutionary Strategies to Nurture Your Child's Developing Mind* by Daniel J. Siegel and Tina Payne Bryson

- *Raising Your Spirited Child: A Guide for Parents Whose Child Is More Intense, Sensitive, Perceptive,*

Persistent and Energetic by Mary Sheedy Kurcinka

- *The Highly Intuitive Child: A Guide to Understanding and Parenting Unusually Sensitive and Empathic Children* by Catherine Crawford

Websites:

- HighlySensitiveKids.com - Provides articles, resources and support for parents of Highly Sensitive Children.

- PsychologyToday.com - Offers various articles and blog posts on Highly Sensitive Children and related topics.

- The HSP Blog - Dr. Elaine Aron's blog is dedicated to highly sensitive people, including children.

- ParentingforBrain.com - Features tips and strategies for parenting Highly Sensitive Children, including energy management techniques.

Other Resources:

- Podcasts: Look for podcasts that focus on parenting, mindfulness and topics related to Highly Sensitive Children.

- Support Groups: Consider joining online or local support groups for parents of Highly Sensitive Children to connect with others facing similar challenges and share resources.

- Online Courses: Explore online courses or workshops on mindfulness, parenting and supporting Highly Sensitive Children.

- Dr. Elaine Aron's The Highly Sensitive Person: How to Thrive When the World Overwhelms You.

- A blog on "Raising an Empathetic Child: Tips and Strategies for Parents" by Parenting Empaths.

- Try this podcast: Sensitive Souls: Parenting Highly Sensitive Children hosted by Sensitive Souls.

Articles:

- Understanding and Nurturing Your Highly Sensitive Child by Psychology Today

- The Highly Sensitive Child: What to Know by Child Mind Institute

- How to Help Your Highly Sensitive Child by Verywell Family

- Highly Sensitive Children: The Challenge of Parenting Sensory-Processing Sensitivity by ADDitude Magazine

- The Top 10 Survival Tips for Parents of Highly Sensitive Children by Hey Sigmund

REFERENCES

Chawla, L. (2020). Childhood nature connection and constructive hope: A review of research on connecting with nature and coping with environmental loss. *People and Nature*, *2*(3), 619–642. https://doi.org/10.1002/pan3.10128

Dutcher, J. M., Creswell, J. D., Pacilio, L. E., Harris, P. R., Klein, W. M. P., Levine, J. M., Bower, J. E., Muscatell, K. A., & Eisenberger, N. I. (2016). Self-Affirmation activates the ventral striatum. *Psychological Science*, *27*(4), 455–466. https://doi.org/10.1177/0956797615625989

Eisenberg, N., Eggum, N. D., & Di Giunta, L. (2010). Empathy-Related Responding: Associations with Prosocial Behavior, Aggression, and Intergroup Relations. *Social Issues and Policy Review*, *4*(1), 143–180. https://doi.org/10.1111/j.1751-2409.2010.01020.x

Gu, R., Jing, Y., Yang, Z., Huang, Z., Wu, M., & Cai, H. (2018). Self-affirmation enhances the processing of uncertainty: An event-related potential study. *Cognitive, Affective, & Behavioral Neuroscience*, *19*(2), 327–337. https://doi.org/10.3758/s13415-018-00673-0

Jacka, F. N., Kremer, P., Berk, M., De Silva-Sanigorski, A. M., Moodie, M., Leslie, E., Pasco, J. A., & Swinburn, B. (2011). A Prospective study of diet quality and mental health in adolescents. *PloS One*, *6*(9), e24805. https://doi.org/10.1371/journal.pone.0024805

Janssen, I., & LeBlanc, A. G. (2010). A systematic review of the health benefits of physical activity and fitness in school-aged children and youth. *the International Journal of Behavioural Nutrition and Physical Activity*, *7*(1), 40. https://doi.org/10.1186/1479-5868-7-40

Kilmer, R. P. (2006). Resilience and Posttraumatic Growth in Children. In L. G. Calhoun & R. G. Tedeschi (Eds.), Handbook of posttraumatic growth: Research & practice (pp. 264–288). Lawrence Erlbaum Associates Publishers.

Kirwil, L. (2009). Parental mediation of children's internet use in different European countries. *Journal of Children and Media*, *3*(4), 394–409. https://doi.org/10.1080/17482790903233440

Lichenstein, S. D., Verstynen, T., & Forbes, E. E. (2016). Adolescent brain development and depression: A case for the importance of connectivity of the anterior cingulate cortex. *Neuroscience & Biobehavioral Reviews/Neuroscience and Biobehavioral Reviews*, *70*, 271–287. https://doi.org/10.1016/j.neubiorev.2016.07.024

Masten, A. S. (2011). Resilience in children threatened by extreme adversity: Frameworks for research, practice, and translational synergy. *Development and Psychopathology*, *23*(2), 493–506. https://doi.org/10.1017/s0954579411000198

Masten, A. S., & Tellegen, A. (2012). Resilience in developmental psychopathology: Contributions of the Project Competence Longitudinal Study. *Development and Psychopathology*, *24*(2), 345–361. https://doi.org/10.1017/s095457941200003x

O'Keeffe, G. S., & Clarke-Pearson, K. (2011). The impact of social media on children, adolescents, and families. *Pediatrics*, *127*(4), 800–804. https://doi.org/10.1542/peds.2011-0054

Sentenac, M., Arnaud, C., Gavin, A., Molcho, M., Gabhainn, S. N., & Godeau, E. (2011). Peer victimization among school-aged children with chronic conditions. *Epidemiologic Reviews*, *34*(1), 120–128. https://doi.org/10.1093/epirev/mxr024

Sherman, R. (2017). *To love a Highly Sensitive Person: A theoretical study on romantic relationships and sensitivity.* https://doi.org/10.15760/honors.391

Smith, P. K., Mahdavi, J., Carvalho, M., Fisher, S., Russell, S., & Tippett, N. (2008). Cyberbullying: its nature and impact in secondary school pupils. *Journal of Child Psychology and Psychiatry and Allied Disciplines*, *49*(4), 376–385. https://doi.org/10.1111/j.1469-7610.2007.01846.x

Tsao, L., Davenport, R. B., & Schmiege, C. J. (2011). Supporting Siblings of Children with Autism Spectrum Disorders. *Early Childhood Education Journal*, *40*(1), 47–54. https://doi.org/10.1007/s10643-011-0488-3

About the Author

Millie Thornfield is a dedicated Family and Psychology Counselor and lives with her husband and three children in Michigan. With a passion for guiding individuals toward understanding and growth, Millie has built a diverse toolkit as a multispecialist therapist. She seamlessly blends various therapeutic approaches to address her clients' cognitive, emotional, and behavioral needs.

Whether working one-on-one or in group settings, Millie's approach is grounded in empathy and a genuine desire to help people navigate life's challenges. She is particularly known for her work with neurodivergent children, and her sessions are more than just therapy—they're a space for clients to explore their thoughts and emotions safely, to make sense of their experiences, and to find a path forward. Millie's belief in the resilience of the human spirit shines through in her work, as she helps each person she meets to discover their strength and potential.

Millie has now embarked on a new journey as an author. Drawing from her extensive experience in therapy and her deep understanding of human behavior, Millie shares her insights in a way that is both accessible and inspiring. Her writing brings her professional knowledge to a broader audience, offering readers practical tools and compassionate guidance to navigate their emotional and psychological landscapes. Through her words, Millie hopes to make a difference beyond her practice, helping more people find clarity, healing, and growth in their everyday lives.

At home, Millie is happiest surrounded by her family, who keep her life in balance and remind her of the importance of connection and understanding. Her work and her family life are woven together by the same thread: a commitment to fostering well-being and nurturing relationships. Millie's presence in both her practice and her home is one of warmth, wisdom, and unwavering support.

Also Published by Phoenix ePublishing

Improve Your Life Skills series

The Essential Beginners Guide to Meditation and Mindfulness
by Rohini Heendeniya

A comprehensive guide that introduces readers to the concepts and practice of meditation and mindfulness. The big idea behind this book is that anyone can learn to meditate, regardless of their background or beliefs, and that incorporating mindfulness into daily life can have profound effects on well-being.

The Essential Beginners Guide to Buddhism
by Rohini Heendeniya

In this blueprint to life, learn that the philosophy of Buddhism is not about blind faith; it is about active practice and a transformative personal experience. It offers pragmatic approaches to self-understanding and provides practical tools to navigate your way through. This compassionate approach has the potential to catalyze profound healing and growth.

The Happy Couple Blueprint
by Rohini Heendeniya

Discover the incredible results that await you when you unleash your love relationship potential with emotional intelligence. Develop effective communication strategies, manage conflicts in a healthy way, and create harmony and happiness in your relationship with this must-read guide.

The Happy Couple Blueprint Companion Workbook & Journal
by Rohini Heendeniya

This Companion Workbook & Journal supports the activities in The Happy Couple Blueprint and keeps you moving toward your goals and helps you build strong bonds with your partner. Here's where you learn how to communicate effectively with your partner; understand yourself and each other on a deeper level.

Forgiveness Unchained
by Rohini Heendeniya

A profound book that centers on the idea of forgiveness as a powerful tool for personal healing and growth. It explores the psychological, emotional, and spiritual aspects of forgiveness, offering practical strategies to overcome past hurts and move toward emotional well-being.

Spiritual Skills series

Tarot Reference Guide, Workbook & Journal
by Maya Quinn

The perfect one-stop journal for Tarot practitioners to develop their intuition and awareness. A guide to the meanings, spreads, and a prompted Journal to create a readings record to deepen their practice.

Phoenix Classics series

The Prophet
by Kahlil Gibran
Introduction by C K Fleming

A 20th Century classic of beguiling and captivating inspirational poems, together with the author's own original illustrations. Included is an introduction to this extraordinary author, setting out his unusual life and the influences that helped develop his timeless work.

Tales From Shakespeare
by Charles and Mary Lamb
Introduction by C K Fleming

This celebrated collection from twenty of Shakespeare's most well-known comedies and tragedies, have allowed children and adults to enjoy and appreciate these wonderful stories. The tales have been adapted from the original plays without losing any of their enjoyment and power.

The Metamorphosis
by Franz Kafka
Introduction by C K Fleming

From one of the most influential authors of the 20th Century, this classic absurdist novella delves into the depths of the human psyche, a thought-provoking and darkly comic exploration of identity and alienation.

Little Women
by Louisa May Alcott
Introduction by C K Fleming

The classic story of four sisters, growing up toward the end of the American civil war, and beloved by generation after generation of young girls ever since its original publication, for its heart, warmth and humor.

What Katy Did & What Katy Did at School
by Susan Coolidge
Introduction by C K Fleming

The evergreen classic of the adventures of a feisty and unconventional 12-year-old girl growing up in 1870s small town America. Generations of girls have loved her and been inspired by her journey to adulthood. Here in one volume are the first two and most popular of the books about Katy.

Made in the USA
Columbia, SC
24 March 2025

55650860R00096